All You Need to Know about

Accounting and Accountants

A Student's Guide to Careers in Accounting

ROBERT LOUIS GROTTKE

ISBN: 1492283673
ISBN 13: 9781492283676

Library of Congress Control Number: 2013915876
CreateSpace Independent Publishing Platform
North Charleston, South Carolina

Also by Robert L. Grottke

All I Needed to Know in Life I Learned
Selling Door to Door

To All My Children, Grandchildren and Great Grandchildren,

Whom I Love Very Much

Index

Acknowledgements

This book reflects the criticisms and support of many of my former business associates, friends, children, grandchildren, students and others to whom I owe my gratitude. Many of these people spent a significant amount of time helping make this effort better.

The author wishes to thank particularly Dan Doherty, Stan Logan, Jim Norris, Gregory Trompeter, Gary Grottke,Tom Grottke, Hall Evans, Laurie Mandich, Melva and Ed Madsen (formerly Melva Gage) and Dick Bragaw.Special thanks also goes to Ron Gavrilovic who was very helpful in the technical production of the prepublished manuscript.

Also, last but not least, to my ever suffering wife, who put up with constant conversations, discussions and redrafts of this book until its final publication and who also made many helpful suggestions.

Robert Louis Grottke

Introduction

This book is about the basic fundamentals of accounting. It describes the function of accounting and its purpose. It is a primer, directed to students just beginning to study accounting and those who are deciding whether they should. It should also be useful for mature individuals with non-accounting or non-financial backgrounds who wish to gain some understanding of accounting. The purpose of this book is not only to introduce the student to the concepts and principles of accounting, but also to answer the question, what does an accountant or auditor actually do, and do I think I would like to do that. The book is directed to accounting for commercial enterprises, therefore it excludes governmental accounting.

This book was conceived when it became apparent from the personal experience of my daughter, Gwen, while in college, that young students (defined as those who have never left school to gain work experience) can sometimes be at a competitive disadvantage in the classroom because they must compete with older students who have some experience in the workplace. This book is also intended to level the playing field for the young students, by providing a clear and concise description of the fundamentals of accounting, auditing and financial reporting, together with a brief listing of definitions of selected key accounting and financial terms.

The book does not cover more advanced accounting pronouncements of the Financial Accounting Standards Board (FASB) issued to direct accountants how to account for various types of transactions. Nor does it cover regulations issued by the Securities and Exchange Commission –SEC (the governmental body that regulates the sales of stocks and bonds to the public) on how financial statements should be filed with the SEC.

There are several different types or levels of accountants. There are accounting clerks or bookkeepers who may have taken a bookkeeping course in high school, or some college level courses. These accountants may reconcile bank statements, prepare sales or billing invoices, maintain detailed perpetual inventory records or perform other similar tasks. They can also maintain accounting records commonly referred to as "books." They may also prepare various financial reports..

Then there are accountants who possess more advanced skills, having usually studied accounting at the college level or equivalent. There are two designations of accountants over and above a " plain" accountant. A public accountant who is licensed by a state and is allowed to use the designation PA for Public Accountant or LPA for Licensed Public Accountant. Most states have discontinued this practice opportunity.

The highest level of accountant is a Certified Public Accountant (CPA) This is achieved by studying accounting, auditing and law courses, obtaining a Bachelors Degree and in most states attending college for at least a fifth year. The candidate must pass the Uniform Certified Public Accounting Examination, which is set by the American Institute of Certified Public Accountants and administered by the National Association of State Boards of Accountancy.

A person who passes this examination is eligible to receive a CPA certificate from the state in which the exam was taken. To practice as an audit partner in a CPA firm, a person needs a CPA certificate and a state license. The license may require a certain number of years of experience. Accountants who work for an individual company (not a CPA firm) do not normally need a state license.

To illustrate various documents and reports associated with accounting, a fictitious company – XYZ Company, Inc. has been developed to illustrate these reports..

The opinions in this book are those of the author based on his personal experience and may not necessarily be in concert with opinions of others.

This book is in no way intended as a replacement or substitute for the accounting text books used by college students who study accounting. This book is a brief but comprehensive overview of the accounting profession intended to introduce the student to the subject and to provide some guidance as to what an accountant or auditor actually does. The intent is to provide the student some information on the subject to help them decide if they want to study accounting and possible become an accountant as their chosen profession.

Robert Louis Grottke

CHAPTER ONE

Accounting – A Scorekeeping System

In order to understand the profession of accounting, or public accounting as the profession calls itself, it is helpful to consider the basic meaning of the word "accounting." Per Webster's dictionary, accounting is "the system of recording and summarizing business and financial transactions in books and analyzing, verifying and reporting the results." A more detailed definition is accounting is a discipline involving preparation and maintenance of records of financial transactions to facilitate preparation of various reports for all types of organizations including businesses, not-for-profits and governmental bodies.

It can be likened to scorekeeping. For example, while the ball may be hit back and forth in tennis for practice, once a game is started, the score is kept to determine (account for) who wins or loses the game. Baseball is a somewhat better example in that in addition to the score of the game, there is a box score which has statistics on each batter and each pitcher. The box score lists at bats, hits, runs scored, errors, runs batted in and batting average. Pitching statistics include innings pitched, hits and runs allowed.

In the business world, accounting is the practice of keeping score to determine how a business is performing. Is the business making a profit or is it losing money? Accounting measures the revenue and costs over a period of time and the related effect on the businesses' assets and liabilities. Similar to a baseball box score, accountants also produce additional financial and operating data so that management can gain insight into the various aspects of the operations of the enterprise. These supplemental reports are sometimes called Key Performance Indicators or KPIs.

What Accounting Measures

Accounting measures or accounts for five types of items or activities as follows;

- -Revenues or income
- -Costs and expenses
- -Assets
- -Liabilities
- -Stockholders Equity or Net Worth

Revenues include sales, billings, service fees, interest income, etc. Costs and expenses include the cost of products sold, wages and salaries, payroll taxes, rents, insurance, supplies, utilities, repairs and maintenance, interest expense, etc.

An asset represents something of value such as cash, inventory, supplies, equipment, machinery, land, buildings, trucks, etc. These are tangible assets. There are also intangible assets, such as patents, copyrights, software and other types of intellectual property. Liabilities include obligations to pay someone or some entity for items purchased, services rendered or money borrowed.

For corporations, Stockholders Equity or Net Worth consists of Common Stock plus retained earnings or less net deficit. Other items which may or may not be included in stockholders equity are Preferred Stock and Paid in Capital. (Capital represents funds paid into the entity.) Repurchased stock called Treasury Stock, if any, is deducted from Shareholders Equity. For entities other than corporations, net worth simply consists of owners capital (funds invested in the business) plus retained earnings or less losses.

Accounting measures revenues and expenses over time periods such as months or years. These time periods are sometimes referred to as fiscal periods. It also provides a snapshot of the value of an enterprise or business at a given moment of time, by measuring or accounting for the value of the assets less the liabilities. The difference between the assets and liabilities is the net worth or net deficit of the business.

The measurement or accounting for revenue and expenses is known as the "profit and loss statement" or simply the "Income statement." The measurement of the assets, liabilities and net worth or deficit at a given date is called the "balance sheet."

Other enterprises, such as not-for-profit organizations and governments are also subject to accounting and accountability. Accounting can also be used to measure the financial activities of an individual person or a family. Income measured would include wages, interest on bank deposits or bonds, dividends, pension and social security payments, etc. Expenses would be all living expenses such as mortgage or rent payments, utilities, food and clothing, insurance, car payments, entertainment, etc.

Accounting Records

Accounting involves a systematic approach to maintaining records in which to accumulate and total the various activities to be measured. This is sometimes referred to as bookkeeping. A series of records is developed to record and accumulate (measure) the various financial activities. Records are kept and reports prepared in accordance with Generally Accepted Accounting Principles commonly referred to as GAAP.

The basic item in an accounting system is a transaction, which is a single event such as a sale, a purchase, or a cash receipt or a cash disbursement. Transactions are accumulated in an organized manner in the supporting accounting system, The resulting data is then used to prepare financial and operating reports, as well as tax returns and other reports required by various governmental regulatory agencies.

Financial Statements Produced

Accountants produce internal financial and operating statements to provide management with information required to run the business. Internal statements means reports used only by management and employees. Besides the profit and loss statement and the balance sheet, supplemental data, similar to the box score of the baseball game, is also produced. For example, operating results of divisions or factories, expense ratios to sales, sales increases or decreases by location, cost of units produced, gross profit by department and average sale per customer.

External financial statements are provided to shareholders, owners, banks and others who may have loans to the enterprise or in the case of companies whose stock is wholly or partially held by the public, to the

Securities and Exchange Commission (SEC). The SEC was created in 1934 to regulate the sale of securities, both stocks and bonds(i.e. debt obligations)to the public. Public company shares are listed on a stock exchange such as the New York Stock Exchange or the NASDAQ. Their shares may be purchased by individuals, by mutual funds, by hedge funds and by pension funds.

External Financial Statements also have a series of attached footnotes describing various aspects of the business, its accounting conventions, and well as displaying supplemental information. Much of this information is required by the SEC.

CHAPTER TWO

Mechanics of Accounting

The function of accounting is facilitated by an organized system of record keeping. While this has changed over time, particularly by the advent of computers notably PCs,(Personal Computers) the fundamentals haven't changed. This chapter is a rather detailed description of the accounting systems needed to accumulate data required for the preparation of various reports

The system begins by accumulating in an organized manner various transactions. A transaction can be described as a single event, such as a sale, purchase or a cash receipt. For example, years ago, when kids set up a lemonade stand in the neighborhood, the sale of a single glass of lemonade for say $.10, was a transaction.

Transactions are generally evidenced by various documents. Sales by sales invoices, purchases by vendor invoices, expenses by expense invoices, cash receipts by remittance advices or deposit slips and cash disbursements by checks. The preparation of these documents is generally performed by accounting staff. The larger the company or the more numerous the transactions, the more accounting staff is required.

Recording Transactions

The Initial recording of various transactions from the supporting documents is usually to a file called a journal. Following is a listing of various types of journals

-sales
-purchases
-payroll
-expenses
-cash receipts
-cash disbursements
-general

These journals would be further segregated by type. For example, in a department store, sales would be accumulated by department, for example cosmetics, ladies clothing, men's clothing, household furnishings, etc.

Accumulations are usually done for a month at a time. At the end of the month, the total of each journal is posted (listed) to an account called a ledger account. An account is a record where similar transactions are listed and accumulated. Examples are cash, inventory, sales, utilities, travel, etc. The totals of all accounts are maintained in a ledger, called a general ledger. In modern accounting systems supported by computers, many transactions are posted directly to the ledger accounts, rather than to the journals.

The general ledger is the basic document or key record in any accounting system. All transactions are recorded in the general ledger either in detail or in summary totals from the journals. This is generally called posting in accounting lingo.

Chart of Accounts

Accounts are usually assigned a series of numbers, which are listed in a "chart of accounts." Numbers are usually assigned on a schematic basis. For example, 100s for assets, 200s for liabilities, 500's for net worth accounts, 600s for revenues, and 700s and 800's for costs and expenses and 900 for interest expense. All transactions are coded with the applicable account numbers per the chart of accounts. The coded documents are then recorded into the appropriate accounts For example, using XYZ Company's chart of accounts, a hotel invoice would be coded 845 for travel and 301 for accrued expense. See Appendix Two for an illustration of XYZ Company's chart of accounts.

Debits and Credits

In an accounting sense, all transactions have two sides to them. For example, a sale is either paid for in cash or is billed to customer. So while the sale is a revenue account, the offset is an equal amount to an asset account -- either cash or accounts receivable. This dual recording is called double entry bookkeeping. The two sides of each recorded transaction are referred to as debits and credits. The debits must always equal the credits, so the "books balance." All assets , costs and expenses are recorded as debits, while all liabilities and revenues or income are recorded as credits.

Transactions can either increase the balance in an account or decrease it, depending on the type of transaction. For example, a cash sale increases cash , while an expense payment decreases it. As an illustration, assume a cash sale of $100 and an expense payment of $50. Using a concept called T-Accounts, which is a visual depiction of an account, these transactions are illustrated below;

Cash		Sales		Expense	
Debits	Credits	Debits	Credits	Debits	Credits
(1) $100	(2) $50		(1) $100	(2) $50	

Accounts can either accept debits or credits. Visually, debits are always on the left side of an account while credits are on the right side. In this example, in the first transaction, cash is debited (an increase) and sales are credited (also an increase.)

In the second transaction, expense is debited (an increase) while cash is credited (a decrease.)

In summary, debits increase assets, costs and expenses, and credits decrease them. Credits increase liabilities, sales and revenues and net worth accounts, while debits decrease them.

When an incurred expense is posted to an expense account, the offset is either a cash payment, which is a reduction of the cash asset, or an increase in accounts payable. In this case, the debit is the expense and the equal credit is a reduction in cash or an increase in accounts payable. Accounting records are often referred to as "books." Each accounting entry consists of equal dollar amounts of debits and credits.

Monthly Trial Balance

At the end of each month, a listing of all of the accounts in the general ledger is prepared. It is called a trial balance, because the total of the debits must equal the total of the credits so that the trial balance balances. If it doesn't, it indicates an error must have been made somewhere, and the accounts must be checked until the error is found and corrected. In addition, some of the accounts may need to be adjusted for various reasons. The monthly profit and loss statement and balance sheet is then prepared from the adjus balance of the accounts.

Another aspect of accounting systems is how longer-term assets are accounted for. For example, a manufacturing plant, a warehouse or a piece of equipment is first recorded as an asset. The accountant then estimates how long the plant or equipment will last. This is referred to as the estimated useful life of the asset. The use of the asset in the business operation is then charged to expense ratably over its useful life. This expense (typically called a write- off) is called depreciation. For example, a piece of equipment purchased for say $10,000 with an estimated useful life of 10 years, is depreciated $1000 per year over the ten-year period,

This transaction is recorded as a debit for depreciation expense and a credit to an account called reserve for depreciation. The reserve account is basically a valuation reserve and is reported as a reduction of the asset on the balance sheet. At the end of five years the presentation of the asset and the reserve for depreciation would be shown on the balance sheet as follows;

Equipment	$10,000
Reserve for Depreciation	$(5000)

Long term assets are always recorded at historical cost (the actual cost in dollars at the time the asset was purchased) and therefore, after a period of time, the current value or market value may exceed the recorded cost on the books, due to inflation.

Matching Revenues with Expenses

One of the functions of accounting is to spread the value of an item over the period to which it applies rather than recording it all in the period when it was paid. This concept is called matching revenues with expenses. For example, a sale or revenue item may be paid for at one time, but may cover an extended period. A season ticket holder must pay for the ticket in advance, however, it entitles the holder to attend all the games or functions played over the season. The players are paid on a game by game or monthly basis. Other expenses such as utilities, ticket takers, security personnel, etc. are also paid each month. Therefore, the revenue from the season ticket sales must be spread over the whole season.

When the cash is received from the season ticket holders, the transaction is recorded as a debit to cash and a credit to an account called "Deferred Season Ticket Revenue." When the season starts and games are played, a pro-rata portion of the Deferred Season Ticket Revenue is allocated to each months' games. Single game ticket sales would be recorded in the appropriate month in which the game was played. This spreading of the deferred season ticket revenue is referred to as amortization.

Amortization can apply to either revenues or expenses. Revenue items can include rents, maintenance or service contracts, ticket sales etc. While these items are income to the recipient, they are an expense to the payer, and hence would initially be recorded as prepaid ticket costs and be amortized over the applicable period as a charge to expense.

Internal Control

Another very important function of accounting systems is to provide internal controls over the operation of the business to ensure the accuracy of the recording of transactions and the production of related financial statements, as well as safeguarding the assets of the business. This is generally accomplished by segregating duties and responsibilities among employees, by implementing procedures that provide checks and balances and by utilizing an internal audit function. This function may be outsourced or performed by a separate internal audit department

within the company. The head of that department should report directly to the Board of Directors.

For example, cash handling and recording should be allocated among
several employees. Cash receipts should be sent directly to a bank
lockbox by customers. Employees recording cash receipts from remittance advices should not be allowed to perform any function related to
billing and cash disbursements.

Checks should be prepared based on approved vendor invoices, supported by purchase orders and receiving reports, if applicable. Checks
should only be issued to approved vendors. Checks should be signed
or signatures controlled by persons other than check preparers. Large
checks over a fixed dollar amount should require a second signature.

Companies should use a system called positive pay, in which check files
are sent to banks, listing check number, payee and amount, so that when
checks are presented for payment, they are matched to the check register or disbursement file, before being cleared for payment by the bank.

Month-end bank statements should be mailed by the bank directly to
an employee not involved in processing cash receipts or cash disbursements. The employee receiving the bank statements, should reconcile
them promptly each month to the check register and cash balance
recorded on the books..

Organizations should also have internal auditors who review and test
various other functions back to original documents and authorizations.
This should include billing, paying, financial statement preparation and
other functions.

The above listings are simply examples of internal controls. Various
other aspects of the operation of the business should also be subject to
internal controls and internal audits.

CHAPTER THREE

Generally Accepted Accounting Principles

Accountants must maintain records and prepare financial statements in accordance with Generally Accepted Accounting Principles, commonly called GAAP. These principles have generally been established by the accounting profession itself. Currently, there is an organization called the Financial Accounting Standards Board, or FASB that assesses the need for accounting principle updates based on changes in the market and economic trends. They issue pronouncements called FASB bulletins. The FASB is the successor organization to the Accounting Principles Board (APB) which also established accounting principles.

On July 1,2009, the FASB issued FASB Accounting Standards Codification as the sole source of authoritative nongovernmental U. S. Generally Accepted Accounting Principles (GAAP.) The codification was effective for fiscal periods ending after September 15, 2009.

The Securities and Exchange Commission, (SEC), was established in 1934 to regulate the sale of securities (stocks and bonds) to the public. The SEC has generally demurred to the accounting profession to establish accounting principles. It does, however, issue regulations as to what types of financial reports must be made available to the public and how often they must be issued.

Generally, accounting principles are conservative. The old adage is anticipate no gains, recognize all losses. For example, the recording of the revenue from a sale should not be done, until the sale is actually consummated. This usually involves the purchaser actually receiving or taking title to the product or service being sold. Some sales are based on signed contracts specifying delivery and other conditions. Sales should not be recorded based on a promise or vague commitment to buy. In some cases, particularly involving retail store operations, customers have the right of return. In these cases, while the actual sales can be recorded, a reserve should also be set up based on estimates of the number and value of the returns. This reserve should be based on the historical average of returns adjusted for current conditions.

Historical Cost

Accounting records are recorded and maintained in current dollars. This generally works well for current assets such as cash, accounts receivable, inventory and other current assets. However, this results in long-term assets such as buildings, land, plant and equipment often being undervalued due to the effect of inflation. Historical cost, then, usually does not reflect the current market value of long term assets.

One result is that depreciation of long-term assets, does not reserve or accumulate sufficient dollars to replace the related asset when it wears out and needs to be replaced. In addition, pricing of products or services, as related to the underlying costs, maybe lower than required to provide capital in excess of depreciation so that the applicable asset can be purchased when it needs to be replaced.

Cash Versus Accrual Accounting Methods

A significant distinction in accounting methods is Cash versus Accrual. In a Cash method, the only transactions recorded in an accounting period are those paid or received in cash. A cash sale is recorded immediately, whereas a credit sale is not recorded until it is ultimately paid in cash. The same is true for all costs and expenses. Only those items paid in cash or received in cash are recorded in the period for which the accounting is being done.

In an Accrual method, transactions are recorded in the period in which they occur even if they are not paid in cash until a later date. For example, a credit sale is recorded when made, and results in an account receivable for which the cash may not be received until a later date.

Most commercial companies use the Accrual method, because it more accurately reflects the economic activity of the period. . In some cases, the Accrual method is used for internal and external reporting, but the cash method is used for tax purposes. This defers taxes owed on, say Accounts Receivable, until they're actually paid.

Governmental Accounting

Accounting for Federal, state and local governments had historically been on a cash basis. Now, however, accrual or partial accrual accounting has been introduced.

However, governments generally do not prepare balance sheets using commercial GAAP rules. While the US government's balance sheet includes all government bonds and debt instruments, and also has accruals for pensions owed to government employees including the armed services, it has no accruals for what's owed for social security and Medicare.

If it did, for example, they would have to include as liabilities the actuarial amount owed for Social Security and Medicare. Accruals would also have to be made for current workers as they earn the right to those entitlements upon retirement. The actuarial amount owed for social security and Medicare is shown in supplemental schedules, however.

The balance sheet would also show as assets all the federal land, buildings and other assets owned by the government.

Use of Estimates

While many believe that accounting is an exact science, i.e. "balanced to the penny," it isn't. Very often, certain liabilities and sometimes assets need to be estimated. For example, some companies may be involved in litigation for various types of claims. While losses should be recorded when the event that occasioned the loss occurred, litigation can drag on for years before the final amount of loss, if any, is determined. For companies, with multiple lawsuits, reserves for potential loss must be established based on estimates.

Estimates are usually also required for warranty expenses, sales returns, and gift card redemption. Insurance companies need to set aside reserves from collected premiums for claims. Premiums are usually collected long before any claims are paid. In many instances, actuaries are used to determine reasonable amounts for these reserve estimates.

In connection with Accounts Receivable, reserves for uncollectible accounts need to be estimated and recorded, so receivables are stated at net realizable value, which is in accordance with GAAP. These reserves are usually based on historical experience, customer data, and to some degree hindsight.

Cost Accounting

Another significant area of accounting is cost accounting. This is generally applied to determine the cost of a product or service, or of a function, such as accepting a manufacture coupon in the supermarket. Cost accounting generally involves both fixed and variable costs. Variable costs are sometimes also referred to as incremental costs.

For example, when manufacturing a product, the raw material used and the direct labor required are variable costs. The more product that is made, the more these costs increase, whereas factory overhead is a fixed cost. Overhead or burden as it is sometimes called includes facilities cost such as rent or depreciation, indirect labor such as receiving, shipping, accounting,taxes, insurance, etc. While these relatively fixed costs may be allocated to the product, they do not generally increase or decrease due to the volume of products produced.

When a manufacturer's product coupons are redeemed by a customer in a supermarket, the manufacturer reimburses the retailer for the face amount of the coupon, plus a handling fee which currently is eight cents per coupon. This handling fee is based on a series of cost accounting studies updated over the years, of the cost of the function of accepting the coupon from the customer at the point-of-sale, and the subsequent processing of the coupon -- counting, sorting, and submitting it to the appropriate manufacturer for reimbursement..

Other functions that maybe the subject of cost accounting include delivery of products purchased, cost of processing a check by a bank, costs related to making a loan, cost of dispensing a prescription, cost per mile of transporting a passenger in a plane or a train, etc.

As you can see, cost accounting is an important function in most businesses. For a business to survive, it must sell its products or services above their cost. So cost accounting is typically employed to determine required selling prices.

CHAPTER FOUR

Financial and Operating Reports

The primary purpose of maintaining accounting records is to facilitate reports, which are used by various constituencies to assess the performance and current status of the business, governmental body or not-for-profit entity. There are three main financial reports generally produced by most businesses, They are the income (profit and loss) statement, the balance sheet and the cash flow statement

The income statement accumulates all revenues and income items, as well as all costs and expenses. The net result is either a profit or a loss. The statement (also referred as the earnings statement or statement of operations), is usually prepared each month, or in some cases each calendar quarter. Small companies may have only one such statement. But larger companies may have many such statements i. e. one for each division, or each plant, or each subsidiary, or each country, or each store. The individual income statements are then consolidated into a total one for the whole company.

Income statements are prepared for members of management in order for them to oversee the operation of the enterprise and take corrective action if goals are not met. Income statements are usually prepared on a comparative basis, showing current year versus prior year. This allows the reader to asses key trends, such as are sales increasing or decreasing. or is the gross profit as a percent to sales increasing or decreasing. A significant decrease in gross profit percent would indicate less profitability on sales, which is a negative trend.

See illustration One for an example of an Income statement for the XYZ Company, Inc.

Another calculation which is made from the income statement is EBITDA, which stands for Earnings before Interest, Taxes, Depreciation and Amortization. EBITDA indicates a company's earning power, exclusive of charges based on sources of capital (interest), tax rates and charges for longer term assets (depreciation and amortization.) It allows comparisons of earning power of different companies.

Another statement prepared from the underlying records is the balance sheet. This is a statement listing all the assets and all the liabilities and shareholders' or owners' equity, as of a given date usually month-end. The total of the liabilities is deducted from the total of the assets, and the difference is the net worth or net deficit of the enterprise. The shareholders' investment in the form of common and/or preferred stock, paid- in capital and retained earnings is included in the net worth of the business.

When reviewing the balance sheet, one of the key items is the excess of current assets over current liabilities, which is called working capital. This is a good indicator of the ability of the entity to pay its bills. Another key ratio is debt to equity or net worth. This generally refers to long term debt, not current liabilities. The lower the ratio (the less debt as a percentage of equity) the more sound the financial position of the entity.

See Illustration Two for an example of a Balance sheet for the XYZ Company Inc. Not- for-profits and governments also usually prepare balance sheets.

The last report is the cash flow statement. Since the income statement contains many non-cash items such as sales on credit, purchases on credit, accruals for unpaid but incurred expenses, the cash flow statement converts or adjusts these non-cash items to calculate what the effect on cash would be.. The cash flow statement also accounts for the cash effect of balance sheet changes such as reduced accounts receivable because cash collections increased, or vice versa, where cash is reduced because receivables increased. In summary, all the effects of cash transactions are summarized in the cash flow statement to determine or account for the increase or decrease in cash for the fiscal period covered by the income statement.

The cash flow statement shows the amount spent for purchases of fixed assets such as plant and equipment, payments on long term debt or increased borrowing of long term debt. It also shows amounts paid out for dividends, or repurchases of its common or preferred stock. Proceeds of any new stock sales would also be shown. In summary, all the major financial transactions of the entity are shown in this statement.

		Current Year	Prior Year		
					Illustration One
	XYZ Company, Inc				
	Statement of Income for the Years ended December 31				
	(In thousands of Dollars)				
Revenues					
Products		$759,321	$689,450		
Services		310,415	290,651		
Financing		21,342	19,695		
Total Revenue		$1,091,078	$999,796		
Costs					
Products		$469,640	$430,876		
Services		229,707	209,268		
Financing		12,232	10,985		
Total Costs		$711,579	$651,129		
Gross Profit		$379,499	$348,667		
Expenses					
Selling, General and Admin		$227,676	$216,342		
Research and Development		6,757	5,936		
Interest		19,232	22,136		
Amortization of Intangibles		2,017	2,159		
Total Expenses		$255,682	$246,573		
Earnings before Taxes		$123,817	$102,094		
Income Taxes		37,145	26,544		
Net Income		$86,672	$75,550		

				Illustration Two	
		XYX Company Inc			
		Balance Sheets as of December 31			
		(in thousands of dollars)			
		Current	Prior		
Assets		Year	Year		
Current Assets					
Cash		$78,986	$70,695		
Marketable Securities		44,322	32,410		
Accountsa Receivable		155,432	140,139		
Inventories		275,690	269,312		
Other		32,619	26,400		
Total Current Assets		$587,049	$538,956		
Buildings and Equipment		$260,632	$245,712		
Reserve for Depreciation		-43,012	-32,340		
Intangible Assets		22,695	24,712		
Total Assets		$827,364	$777,040		
Liabilities &Shareholders Equity					
Current Liabilities					
Accounts Payable		$182,619	$163,612		
Accrued Expenses		140,654	125,212		
Current Maturities of LTD		$42,619	41,243		
Total Current Liabilities		$365,892	$330,067		
Long Term Debt		$250,619	$290,612		
Other Liabilities		86,442	68,622		
Total Liabilities		$702,953	$689,301		
Shareholders Equity					
Common Stock		$10,000	$10,000		
Retained Earnings		114,411	77,739		
Total Shareholders Equity		$124,411	$87,739		
Total Liab & Share Equity		$827,364	$777,040		

See Illustration Three for an example of a cash Flow Statement for the XYZ Company Inc.

These statements are generally referred to as internal financial statements. External financial statements are usually only prepared quarterly and annually as reports to shareholders. Shareholder reports are supported by footnotes and other financial or operating information not generally needed with internal financial statements.

Additional reports can be categorized as follows;

      -- control reports
      -- productivity reports
      -- information reports

There also are other reports which defy simple classification. Each industry generally produces reports specific to the needs of that industry. For example, hospitals produce and maintain patient records. Retailers maintain out-of-stock reports, and markdown reports. Manufactures keep track of manufacturing defects on quality control issues.

To develop these various reports, additional data is required to be developed or maintained in supplemental records. This data can consist of the number of individual units produced or sold. The number of hours worked, or needed to produce an item, the size of the facility in square feet, or the capacity of the plant. Other units of measure such as pounds or tons, number of linear feet, number of customers, etc. may also have to be accumulated in order to produce the required reports.

		Current Year	Prior Year			Illustration Three
XYZ Company Inc						
Statement of Cash Flow for the Years Ended December 31						
(In thousands of dollars)						
Cash flows from operations						
Net Income		$86,672	$75,550			
Depreciation		10,672	11,042			
Amortization		2,017	2,159			
Changes in balance sheet accounts						
Increase in acounts receivable		-15,293	-10,432			
Increase in Inventory		-6,378	-4,300			
Other asstes		-6,219	2,100			
Increase in accounts Payable		19,007	5,672			
Increase in accrued expenses		15,442	4,321			
Net cash from operations		$105,920	$86,112			
Cash flow from Investments						
Purchase plant Equioment		-$14,920	-$10,675			
Purchase of Marketable Securities		-11,912	-5,672			
Net cash used for Investments		-$26,832	-$16,347			
Cash flow from financing						
Payment of Long Term Debt		-$38,617	-$37,400			
Payment of Dividends		-$50,000	-$40,000			
Increase in other liabilities		$17,820	$2,112			
Net cash flow from financing		-$70,797	-$75,288			
Net cash flow		$8,291	-$5,523			
Cash at begining of year		$70,695	$76,218			
Cash at end of year		$78,986	$70,695			

Control Reports

These reports are used to control the various operations of the business to make sure the assets are not wasted or stolen by fraud or other means.

Receiving Reports

These reports are prepared on the receiving dock or other areas where items purchased for use in the business are physically received.

The quantities received are physically counted or inspected, any damage is noted, and the description of the items received is compared to the items ordered per the purchase order, which is another control document. The receiving report is then forwarded to the accounts payable department for matching with the vendors invoice.

Cash and Sales Report

These reports are used by retailers to account for sales and customer payments. A sales associate from each check out area prepares a report each day. At the end of each day, sales per the register are recorded on the report. The register also accumulates the payments by type -- credit cards, debit cards, checks, cash, coupons, gift cards, food stamps, etc. At the close of the day, a sales audit person, then counts all the payment media by type, and balances it to the register totals, also indicating any over or short. The basic goal is to make sure that all the sales have been paid for and properly recorded.

Shrink and Cutting Loss

When processing raw materials into finished product, it is important to make sure that any anticipated shrink or cutting loss is within the normal range. Cutting loss can also occur in any type of manufacturing process, where raw materials are converted to finished goods. Also, in food processing, when beef or other wholesale meat cuts are processed into retail cuts for sale in markets, or restaurants, a certain amount of shrink is anticipated. Processing reports are prepared to monitor the shrink loss to determine that it's reasonable. Excess shrink loss could indicate bad product or inefficient processing..

Inventory Shortage Reports

In many industries, inventories of various goods or products are maintained. They may be of finished goods, parts, raw materials, subassemblies, etc. Inventory records are usually maintained in units by item. The purpose is to monitor inventory levels and to avoid out-of- stock situations by reordering on a timely basis. Physical inventories are taken periodically during the year, and compared to the book or perpetual inventory, to determine its accuracy and calculate any inventory shortage. If the shortage persists or is significant, corrective action must be taken.

Expense Reports

When employees travel, or entertain customers or clients, they are entitled to be reimbursed for these expenses. Most companies have well-defined travel and expense policies, and either pay per diems or actual expenses incurred, depending on the circumstances. Employees are required to complete expense reports describing the business reason for the expense, the purpose of the travel, and the persons entertained, if any. Supporting receipts must also be attached to the report.

All these reports can be categorized as internal control reports, designed to assure that the assets of the business are safeguarded and that cash resources are effectively controlled.

Productivity Reports

Productivity reports are prepared to determine the efficiency of the business operations. These reports may also be referred to as Key

Performance Indictors or KPI's. Generally productivity reports are produced by dividing output by input. For example, sales per man hour is calculated by dividing total sales for the period by total hours worked for the period. Total manufacturing costs are divided by the number of units produced to develop a production cost per unit. Another example is sales divided by square foot of selling space to determine the efficiency of the facility. In warehouse operations, cases selected for shipment by each man's hours give rise to a cases selected per man-hour calculation. Bonuses or incentive pay is often based on these type of proficiency reports.

Standard Costs

Standard cost accounting systems (systems based on anticipated costs of material, labor and overhead in the manufacturing process) generally apply in manufacturing operations, are also a form of productivity measurement and control. Variances from standards indicate some abnormality. This could signal a decrease in productivity. Unfavorable variances in material costs could indicate too much raw material is being consumed in the manufacturing process. Likewise the same could be indicated by unfavorable variations in direct labor. In today's competitive world, management must always closely monitor productivity to determine that operating goals are being met and that production is being done efficiently. See Chapter Ten for a more detailed explanation of standard costs.

The type of productivity reports produced is unique to each industry. For example, in hospitals, quality of care is more important than productivity, yet some productivity measures may apply, like occupancy rates i. e. the number of beds occupied, compared to the total beds in the hospital. Another productivity measurement might be nursing hours per patient day.

Other examples of other productivity reports are as follows;

Industry	Productivity Report
Mining	Tons mined per man hour
Hotels, Motels	Average Occupancy rates
Restaurants	Meals Served Per Day
Retail Stores	Weekly customer count
	Average sales per customer transaction
Banks	Net interest margin
Electric Utilities	KWH (Kilowatt hours) generated per day
Movies	Revenue per week or per theater

Information Reports

Another group of reports produced by accountants are simply information reports, which provide management with supplemental information they need to effectively run the business. Since revenue is essential to success in almost any business enterprise, a variety of sales reports are produced depending on the industry.

Retailers are particularly focused on sales. Sales per store and increases or decreases in same-store sales, (defined as only stores operated for at least a year) are critical reports for management. Most public retail companies report increases or decreases in same-store sales each quarter. Customer count (the number of customers) is also reported weekly by store to determine trends. Are more customers coming to the store each week, or is the customer count declining. Average sale per customer transaction is another measurement generally tabulated by retailers.

Sales, sales trends, and sales increases or decreases are almost always carefully monitored by most businesses. Sales may be reported by location, by product, by product line, or even by customer.

Another information report is an accounts receivable trial balance. This lists all customer invoices due at given date, usually month-end and balances it to the control account in the general ledger. The accounts are listed by due dates and the number of days past due -- current, 30 days past due, 60 days past due, 90 days past due, etc. Accounting personnel use this report to follow up with customers to make sure they finally pay their bill.

Likewise, a trial balance of unpaid vendor invoices is also prepared at each month end. It is also balanced to the control account in the general ledger to determine that all unpaid invoices are accounted for.

CHAPTER FIVE

Budgets, forecasts and Cash flow statements

Most well-run companies or entities, prepare an annual budget for the next fiscal year. A budget is a forecast or estimate of the operations for the next fiscal year. It is also a planning and control tool. A good budget must be prepared from the bottom up rather than the top down. This means that the lowest level of supervisory personnel should prepare the budget for their department or area of responsibility. A top-down budget is prepared by higher level executives, and literally imposed over lower-level managers and employees. They may not always "buy in" and some aspects may not be reasonable.

The accounting department usually sends out worksheets to every supervisor or department head on which to prepare the annual budget. The worksheet should list all the accounts being budgeted, the prior year budget, and year to date actual amounts. Some budget worksheets also forecast what the actual results will be for the remaining months of the current fiscal year. The budget is usually prepared several months prior to the beginning of the new fiscal year.

Budgets

The budget is usually based on a combination of expected revenues and expenses, as well as estimates of expected changes based on plans or initiatives in place by management. For example, when budgeting occupancy costs, rent may be a fixed amount based on a long-term lease. It may also include costs associated with a new facility expected to come on line in the next fiscal year. Salaries may be budgeted based upon current employees, their current salaries, an estimated average salary increase of X percent. Salaries for planned new hires would be included in the budget. Sales or revenues may be budgeted based upon current levels, plus an anticipated increase based on current growth rates, new marketing or sales initiatives, or price increases

Once all the budget worksheets are completed, they are accumulated in the accounting department, reviewed for obvious errors or omissions, corrected, and a preliminary budget is then prepared.. This is then reviewed by top management. If the budgeted results are unsatisfactory, usually because the result is insufficient net income or even a loss, the budget is critically reviewed, and changes as appropriate are made until an acceptable final budget is achieved. Often, planned initiatives are scaled back, planned personnel additions are postponed, or other corrective action is taken to achieve a satisfactory budget. This process allows management to have a good idea, or at least a plan as to what the company's performance for the next fiscal year, would or should be.

As the next fiscal year unfolds, results for each month are compared to the budget and variances are shown. This allows management to monitor operations on an overall basis, and determine if operating goals are being met. If not, focus can be directed to the problem areas, and corrective action taken

The budget also serves as a control tool in certain areas. For example, if $20,000 is budgeted for travel, the supervisor of that area knows that no travel over and above that amount should be approved, without spe-cific permission from higher management.

Forecasts

A forecast is a prediction of the operating results of an entity over a period of time, usually 3 to 5 years. It is based on a series of assumptions. It may reflect some planned strategic changes to the normal operations of the business. It may be an illustration of the anticipated operating results of a new business. It may simply forecast anticipated results of an existing business in the future.

The assumptions upon which the forecast is based are spelled out in detail so the reader can determine what the forecast is based upon. Forecasting can also be used to model the effects of changes in various assumptions. Computers can be used to develop the forecasts based on various changes in assumptions. This allows comparisons of results based on different assumptions.

Forecasts can also be used to model the effect of a proposed merger or acquisition or a new business plan. These type forecasts are generally referred as pro-forma financials. They purport to show the anticipated effect of a potential merger, acquisition or new business plan. The pro-forma financials are based on a series of assumptions which must be spelled out to support the financial projections.

Cash Flow Statements

A cash flow statement converts an income statement from an accrual basis to a cash basis. It also calculates the effect of cash transactions that only affect balance sheet items such as new loans, purchases of fixed assets, and decreases or increases in accounts receivable, inventories or accounts payable. See Chapter Four Illustration Three for an example of a cash flow statement.

Budgets, forecasts, and pro-forma financials should also include cash flow statements. These statements can be used to highlight cash needs associated with new business ventures or pro-forma plans.

CHAPTER SIX

Auditing

One of the most important functions performed by accountants is auditing. Auditing is defined as an examination of something performed or developed by someone else to determine its validity. It's basically scrutinizing something to see if it's true or factual. In an accounting sense, auditing is applied to a set of financial statements, to determine if they are reasonably accurate, or fairly present the information contained in them. There are basically three types of audits;

-audits of various types of company's or entities' financial statements, by independent public accountants

-Internal audits of individual companies or entities accounting and reporting procedures, assets and liabilities

special-purpose audits to detect fraud or to audit areas where fraud is suspected. Also to audit situations or circumstances to determine if or how something happened. This is sometimes called forensic auditing.

Company or Entity audits

All "public" companies and certain other entities require annual audited financial statements by independent public accountants. A "public" company is defined as one who's common or preferred stocks or bonds are wholly or partially owned by the public. These companies' securities are traded on stock exchanges such as the New York Stock and NASDAQ stock exchanges, Other countries also have their own stock exchanges.

These companies must prepare financial statements in accordance with GAAP and in accordance with regulations issued by the United States Security and Exchange Commission (SEC). The financial statements must be audited annually by a public accounting firm qualified to perform such audits. The objective of the audit is to determine that the financial statements of the company being audited present fairly the results of operations for the year just ended and the financial position as of year end, and that the statements do not contain any material misstatements. A series of audit procedures is followed to accomplish this objective. The audit is completed prior to releasing the financial statements to the public, so that if the auditor finds any errors or required changes to the financial statements or the attached footnotes, the corrections can be made to the financial statements prior to their release to the public..

Preparation of Financial Statements

The primary responsibility for the preparation of the annual financial statements rests with the company and its accounting department, headed by its chief financial officer (CFO.) The primary responsibility of the auditor is to verify the accuracy of the financial statements and render an opinion on them, following auditing standards developed by the Public Company Accounting Oversight Board (PCAOB.) The opinion essentially describes what the auditor did and, if applicable, states that the financial statements" present fairly " the results of operations and the financial position of the company for the year ended a specific date. See Appendix Five for an example of an auditors opinion on financial statements.

The annual financial statements are filed with the SEC on a form 10K. Some companies simply send the form 10K to their shareholders, while others republish the financial information or portions of it in their printed annual report along with the 10K.

Investors, analysts, fund managers and other interested parties receive the financial statements of public companies and study them to determine how a particular company did the previous year. The statements essentially measure the results of the company's performance for the past year. This includes the income statement and the financial position of the company as shown in the balance sheet. One of the key figures reviewed is the net income or loss per outstanding share of common stock.

What do Auditors Do

The next question to be answered is what does an auditor actually do. Auditors must follow a set of audit procedures or guidelines, referred to as generally accepted auditing standards. The auditor must first determine that the accounting and operating procedures in place by the company being audited are effective to properly record and accumulate the underlying transactions. These procedures are generally referred to as "internal controls." If the company does not have effective internal controls, the auditor probably cannot perform an effective audit or render an opinion.

After a spate of inaccurate financial statements of public companies that were "certified" as "present fairly" during the period from 1990 to 2000, Congress passed in 2002 the Sarbanes-Oxley Act. This act sometimes jokingly referred to as the public accountants retirement act, required public accountants to audit internal control procedures related to the preparation of financial statements of public companies and express an opinion on them. See Appendix Six for an example of an auditors' opinion on Internal Controls. This is in addition to auditing the financial statements.

The Act also required CEOs and CFOs to assume greater responsibility for the accuracy of their financial statements and the effectiveness of their internal controls over the preparation of their financial statements. They also are required to issue written opinions regarding these issues in with their published financial statements.

This act has increased administrative costs of public companies, with the deleterious effect of causing some companies to list their shares on stock exchanges of other countries.

After the public accountant assesses the effectiveness of a company's internal controls, an audit program is prepared to detail the various audit procedures to be applied by the auditor in auditing the financial statements. If internal controls are determined to be weak in some area, the auditor will expand the testing procedures in that area.

Audit Procedures

While the auditor may examine the books and records of a company, it is the numbers on the financial statements and the information in the footnotes that the audit is directed to verify. Auditors generally follow the following types of procedures in their audit;

-Obtain written confirmation of various balances directly from outside parties, such as banks, customers, vendors, lawyers, mortgage companies.

-Physically observe various assets or procedures, such as physical inventories

-Test records by obtaining source documents to determine that they have been accurately recorded on the books and records of the company

-Recheck calculations and computations of various accounts such as inventories, supplies, depreciation and amortization

-Use post-year end events to verify various year end balances or footnote information

-Review corporate minutes, contracts, agreements, leases, etc. to determine that various transactions or agreements have been properly authorized or recorded

-Review the work of the company's internal audit department to understand the scope of their work, findings and recommendations and to dovetail their scope with the scope of the internal auditors.

Bank confirmations are sent not only to confirm bank balances, but also to identify any outstanding bank loans, and any operating restrictions imposed on the company by bank loan agreements. Auditing standards require that the auditor confirm directly with customers, any outstanding receivable balances as of year end. Not all balances have to be confirmed, only a representative sample. All differences must adequately be explained. The auditor must also determine if the reserve for uncollectible accounts is adequate to cover any potential losses in collecting accounts receivable.

Liabilities must also be confirmed on a test basis. All significant or large liabilities must be confirmed directly with the vendor, bank, mortgagor, or party owed. All the company's outside attorneys are sent confirmations to determine that any potential or actual liabilities owed or potentially owed by the company have been adequately reserved. Companies subject to multiple lawsuits, such as large retail chains, financial institutions, oil companies, consumer products companies, selected manufacturers such as automobile companies, must record reasonable reserves for the potential cost of pending litigation.

For many companies, particularly retailers or wholesalers, inventories are a major asset. Generally, at least once a year, a physical inventory is taken where all items are physically counted, priced and accumulated to determine that the amount recorded on the books is accurate. Auditing standards require that the auditor attend the taking of the physical inventory to determine that counts being made are accurate. Auditors also may record test counts and compare them to the final count of the inventory. Auditors also compare inventory unit costs to purchase invoices, on a test bases, to verify their accuracy. They may also recheck calculations of individual items (quantity times unit cost) and of total inventory accumulations.

Inventory items must also be reviewed to determine if they are obsolete or quantities are in excess of reasonable sales expectations. Obsolete or excess inventories must be reduced to a net realizable value. Auditors must also verify fixed assets which include retail store buildings, warehouses, manufacturing plants, equipment, vehicles, etc. This is usually done by inspecting invoices contracts ,etc. However, some physical verification is also done.

Tests of Transactions

Auditors also perform tests of transactions. This would include sales orders, vendor purchases, expense invoices. Because these transactions are usually numerous, auditors select random samples of documents on each type of transaction, and examine the underlying documents to determine that the transaction was properly recorded. This is generally referred to as "vouching."

Since PC's are in extensive use by auditors, transaction data bases can be tested in detail to look for usual or outlying transactions. For example, the payroll register can be scanned for any check over a normal or maximum amount. Another example would be to check inventory quantities against sales, to highlight any inventory with low or no sales, which could be considered obsolete or in excess supply.

Auditors also use post fiscal period. transactions to prove up balances at year-end. For example, if an account receivable at year-end is subsequently paid, that generally is proof that it was valid and accurate.

Auditors also read all corporate minutes and major legal documents, such as loan agreements, leases, contracts, etc. to determine that related amounts are properly recorded or paid and that these major transactions have Board of Directors approval. Many of these documents affect a period of years, and auditors simply maintain a copy of them in their work papers, so they can be referred to during each annual audit.

The Board of Directors generally has an audit committee that consists either wholly or with at least three outside directors (not company officers, employees, consultants, suppliers or customers). The auditor meets with the audit committee to discuss the scope of the audit and the results. Auditors may also make suggestions on required improvements to internal controls. These suggestions are also in written documents given to the management of the company and to the audit committee.

Auditors document their work in a collection of documents generally referred to as auditor's work papers. Before personal computers, they were prepared manually. Currently most of the data is maintained on personal computer files. Auditors' work papers are maintained as evidence that the auditor has performed a proper audit in accordance with the standards of the Public Company Accounting Oversight Board.

Auditor Independence Rules

One of the critical issues in the accounting profession is whether or not the outside auditor is "an independent auditor." As the size of public accounting firms has grown to where larger firms have in excess of 100,000 personnel, the application of rules for determining independence has become more complex. While some rules are very specific, the application of others are dependent on a variety of circumstances. Essentially the engagement team (those partners, managers and staff working directly on the client audit) cannot have any conditions which could compromise their independence. Following is a list of some of the key rules for auditor independence;

-No one on the engagement team can own any common or preferred stock or bonds in the client company being audited.

-No one on the engagement team can have a close relative employed by the client company being audited, if the close relative is in a financial role or part of the management team.

-The engagement partner who is the partner in charge of the audit, must be rotated off the account after five years

-All partners in a firm auditing a client company cannot own any securities in that client company

Nevertheless, in spite of all the safeguards, questions of independence still arise from government officials and the public. Audit firms tend to be retained by client companies for long periods of time, sometimes 25 years or more. Naysayer's allege that this can create a cozy relationship that could compromise the auditor's judgment. There is always some discussion that audit firms should be required to rotate off a client account every so many years. This has the disadvantage of increasing the cost both to the client company and the auditor. Also, a new auditor may not be that familiar with the company or the applicable industry, which can adversely affect the quality of the audit.

The issue is not so simple. At the highest level, over and above detailed audit checking and confirmations etc., the auditor basically audits the judgment of the management of a company, generally with regard to complex transactions, or difficult to measure situations. Examples of these areas include potential litigation, potential losses on accounts receivable, quality disputes, patent infringement claims, etc. Management and the audit partner must have a close working relationship, so that management will on a timely basis discuss difficult accounting questions and decisions with the auditor in advance of recording and reporting them to the public or the company's constituency. So independence is really a state of mind to be maintained by the auditor, rather than a physical separation after specified time periods.

Management needs to have a relationship with the auditor of utmost respect and recognition that the auditor represents an unbiased assessment of the situation, more or less like a doctor, advising his patient of the consequences of his or her actions, and what needs to be done to maintain a clean bill of health with regard to the accounting and reporting. On the other hand, auditors cannot be people who simply always say no.

They need to be helpful and provide appropriate guidance to their clients not only to keep them out of trouble, but where possible to suggest appropriate ways for them to accomplish their objectives.

They need to be proactive, keeping the management of their client company abreast of accounting rules and the updates of those rules that could have an effect on the company's reporting and accounting. Constantly switching auditing firms does not make for developing the kind of relationships that are required between company management and its auditor

The Intangible Aspect of Auditing

When auditors audit large companies, most with multiple locations many of which may be international, the amount of detail checking of transactions by the auditor, is oft times infinitesimal compared to the total transactions worldwide. Most companies have a corporate office or headquarters, where accounting information is accumulated and used to prepare the corporate consolidated financial statements. So how can the auditor be assured that the financial statements "present fairly" the financial condition of a company and the results of its operations for the previous year.

There are safeguards relied upon by the auditor. First the CEO and CFO are primarily responsible for the preparation and accuracy of the company's financial statements. An exception would be if the CFO is not a CPA, another officer usually designated as the CAO – Chief Accounting Officer would have that primary responsibility. These responsibilities were codified by Congress in the Sarbanes-Oxley Act. These executives would suffer extreme penalties for any willful manipulation of financial data that could result in significantly inaccurate financial statements reported.

Internal Control Audits

Secondly, auditors are now required to audit the internal controls in place to assure that the companies financial reporting is effective and reasonably accurate, and report any major deficiencies to management, or give a clean bill of health on these controls in their opinion.

Thirdly, companies now have extensive internal audit departments or they have a second outside audit firm to perform various audit procedures year-round to assess the integrity of the financial reporting process.

Nevertheless, there is still the potential risk that something could go wrong, on purpose or by accident. So what else can the auditor do to help assure that the audit will find any major misstatements if they exist, or prove that they don't. Auditors must learn all about the industry in which they work, and gain what is called "industry competence," Once an auditor has that type of competence, he or she has a level of expectation on which to compare the financial results of the company being audited.

For example, if the traditional gross margin in a particular industry is 25%, and the auditor notices the company being audited is reporting a 35% gross margin, a "red light" should flash. While it may be correct with a reasonable explanation, certainly additional audit procedures or focus should be on the area to find out why this number is so far out of line. If the auditor is familiar with an industry, understands its operations, its methods, it's normal financial reporting ratios, it's KPIs,(key performance indicators) he or she can now review the financial statements or components thereof being audited and make mental notes or tabulations on what's reasonable and what is not. These types of critical and knowledgeable assessments provide an additional safeguard against any mistakes or misstatements. The leader in this endeavor has to be a very knowledgeable and experienced audit partner. This is exemplified by the quote" he didn't see the forest for the trees." A good audit partner knows a lot about the forest.

In summary, a critical review of the financial results and financial position of the client company by a knowledgeable auditor is a key component of a quality audit.

Internal audits

Public companies and many non-public companies have an internal audit department. This department's function is to perform audits of various company procedures and financial accounts, to enhance the company's internal control. They usually coordinate their work with the audit scope of the outside auditors.

These departments are completely separate from all other company departments and the head of internal audit usually reports directly to the audit committee of the Board of Directors. Internal auditors perform various tests year-round, and continuously challenge financial and operating management to maintain or improve controls over financial reporting. They also focus on safeguarding corporate assets to make sure they are used for corporate purposes and are controlled to prevent any losses. Internal auditors generally follow procedures, similar to those followed by external auditors. They confirm directly with banks cash account balances. They also selectively confirm balances of accounts receivable and accounts payable, with the customers or vendors. This work is all done on a test basis, although some effort is made to focus on larger balances. Exceptions and differences are appropriately followed up and reconciled.

Internal auditors will also test check various cash disbursements to determine that they are properly supported by vendors invoices, purchase orders, receiving reports and freight bills.

The internal audit function has become more important since the debacles of the recent past..

Special audits

Special audits or investigations as they are sometimes called are usually focused on a particular area of a company or government where something amiss has happened or suspected to have happened. Funds are missing or suspected of being misused. These audits are sometimes referred to as forensic audits.

CHAPTER SEVEN

What Does a Public Accountant Do?

Public accounting firms exist to perform various financial services for for-profit companies, not-for-profit organizations and governmental organizations. These services consist of financial auditing, accounting, tax consultation, tax return preparation, internal control examinations and advisory services, including systems integration, actuarial calculations, profit improvement studies, valuation determinations and business recovery. Public accounting firms are usually organized as LLP's and are owned by the partners, who are generally CPAs.

While the most dominant service public accounting firms provide is auditing of public and nonpublic companies, other services are provided as mentioned above. Tax partners who are involved with tax planning, tax return preparation and assistance to audit personnel regarding tax liabilities of client companies, are usually CPAs. However, they may also be attorneys practicing as accountants.

While the PCAOB limits what services public accounting firms can provide to their audit clients, they can provide most advisory type services to non-audit clients.

Partners and other employees who provide advisory services such as systems consulting, corporate finance, strategic planning, actuarial services, risk assessment, performance improvement, etc. may not be CPAs, but may have other disciplines such as computer skills, engineering, actuarial capability or corporate finance. Their work would be different than that of an auditor, however, this chapter will focus mainly on the work of an auditor.

Financial Audits

One of the most important functions of public accounting firms is to perform an annual audit of a company's financial statements and express an opinion on them. All public companies and most large privately held companies have an annual audit. The overall purpose of the audit is to assure the reader of the company's financial statements that they are reasonably correct and have been prepared in accordance with generally accepted accounting principles, GAAP, applied on a consistent basis from year to year. Public companies financial statements must also be filed with the SEC in a format specified by the SEC (See appendix Five for an example of an auditor's opinion.)

The audit partner in a public accounting firm has the final responsibility for the audit of the financial statements of a company assigned to him or her. These companies are usually referred to as clients. Partners have responsibility to audit several clients each year and are usually assigned clients in the same or similar industries. This way they can achieve industry competence and do a better job of auditing.

There is usually a hierarchy of professionals that perform the audit work. First or second year personnel, audit various areas of the company such as cash, accounts receivable, inventory, accounts payable or accrued expenses. Senior staff closely supervise the junior auditors.. These staff personnel are under the supervision of an audit manager, who plans the work, helps develop the audit program(various steps to be performed) and reviews the work as it is being performed.

The audit partner is in charge of this audit team, and is generally familiar with each one's level of competence, having come up through the ranks himself or herself. The audit partner is responsible for planning the audit, developing the audit program and reviewing the work. He or she acts as a liaison with the clients CFO, reports on progress of the audit and discusses issues and potential audit adjustments.

When the audit is complete, the audit partner discusses results with the client's top management and also with the audit committee of the Board of Directors. The audit partner also signs the audit opinion with the name of his or her firm.

Audits of Internal Controls

Ever since the passage of the Sarbanes-Oxley Act in 2002, in response to several significant misstatements of reported financial results of public companies, auditors of public companies have also been required to audit the internal control over the preparation of financial statements, report any major weaknesses to the Board of Directors, and issue a written opinion on the effectiveness of internal control over the preparation of the Company's financial statements.(See appendix Six for an example of this type of opinion.) Needless to say, this requirement has increased the work that must be performed in public companies by auditors, with the result being an increase in audit fees.

The audit of internal controls over the preparation of the client's financial statements is usually performed by the same audit crew that performs the financial audit. The partner essentially has the same responsibility as with the financial audit. The audit partner generally works closely with the clients CFO to assess and evaluate the various risks that could adversely affect the preparation of the financial statements. The results of these risks assessments, guide the various procedures to be performed in the audit of the company's internal controls. Here is where knowledge of the industry as well as the company's operations, is essential for the audit partner to be effective in the development of the audit program, as well as in its execution.

FASB Opinions

Audit partners must keep up with new rules or opinions that may be issued by the Financial Accounting Standards Board -- FASB. As these rules are issued as FASB bulletins, the auditor should become familiar with them and determine how they might affect any clients he or she handles. Any required implementation should be discussed on a timely basis with the CFO, so that plans can be made as to how and when to implement the required new rules.

Audit partners should also develop close working relationships with client CFOs, so they can act as sounding boards for any unique or challenging accounting issues that may arise. Appropriate discussions and analysis on a timely basis, can help a company avoid improperly recording or reporting challenging transactions. Examples of these kinds of issues would be product recalls, legal claims, and pending acquisitions or dispositions.

As the audit partner is involved with these various areas, he or she can develop into a trusted business advisor to the CFO or even the CEO. These close working relationships can help make the audit process more effective. However, the audit partner must always maintain an independent attitude and can never allow relationships to cloud or adversely affect the overall audit goal that the financials are reasonably accurate and do not in any way contain misstatements.

Tax Consultation and Return Preparation

Public Accounting Firms also have significant tax practices staffed by partners specializing in income tax matters. They assist audit personnel in determining that all income taxes owed by the client are properly recorded and accrued in the financial statements that are the subject of the audit.

Tax partners also consult with clients to discuss ways they can reduce their tax liabilities. They can advise them of changes or planned changes in the tax laws or regulations that may affect their clients tax liabilities. They can assist with IRS investigations of a client's tax returns. Tax partners also prepare and file tax returns for individuals, corporations and partnerships.

Special Projects

In addition to basic accounting and auditing. Public Accountants are often involved in a variety of interesting and challenging projects. These include;

    -systems development and installation
    -mergers and acquisitions
    -profit improvement studies
    -cost accounting projects
    -litigation support and expert witnessing
    -industry studies for trade associations

Following is a brief description of each of these types of projects

Systems Development and Installation

This involves several types of projects including determination of system needs or requirements, analysis of vendor proposals and selection, project management and systems implementation. Public accountants are particularly capable of assistance with accounting and reporting systems, inventory control systems, billing and accounts receivable systems and accounts payable systems. All these systems affect internal controls which is an area of expertise of accountants.

Accountants also have a good knowledge of the types and frequency of reports which are needed by management and can be helpful in the design of the supporting systems and reports. They can also be impartial in helping management in the selection of software packages that would be best suited for their company.

Mergers and Acquisitions

Accountants are often engaged to help companies with mergers and acquisitions. They may be hired to review a potential acquisition's financial statements to obtain certain required financial information or to help determine how the two companies would fit together. Accountants may also be asked to perform certain analysis to help determine the pros and cons of a contemplated merger or acquisition.

Accountants may also be requested to develop pro forma financial statements of the combined operations adjusted for the anticipated financial effects of the combined companied such as administrative savings, increased margins, etc.

They would prepare the pro-forma financials based on assumptions of the savings, increased margins, etc.

Profit Improvement Studies

Companies may try to increase their profits, either by reducing operating costs or by increasing revenues. They often engage public accountants to review and analyze their various operations to determine what cost savings can be made, or how revenues can be increased.

Very often procedures that made sense years ago are still being followed, even though conditions have changed. Therefore, some processes currently being done, may no longer need to be done. Since accountants have to review procedures related to evaluation of internal controls, they develop expertise in this area. This allows them also to evaluate the efficiency of various procedures.

These studies also involve extensive analysis of various types of transactions to assess their effect on profitability. For example, sales orders may be analyzed by size or by type of customer to determine which orders are most profitable. These analyses can lead to adjustments in pricing or a redirection of selling focus in order to improve the overall gross profit on sales.

Cost Accounting Studies

Public accountants are sometimes engaged to perform interesting and challenging cost accounting studies. For example, over a period of 30 years, the consumers packaged goods industry and the grocery retail industry asked accountants to perform a cost accounting study of the handling costs of accepting a manufacturer coupon in a grocery store, sorting them by manufacturer and submitting them back to the issuing manufacturer for reimbursement, currently eight cents a coupon. Coupon issuing manufacturers reimburse retailers who accept coupons, the face amount of the coupon plus the handling fee. At one point, each penny of handling fee resulted in manufacturers paying retailers about $40 million annually.

These studies were initially performed based on sets of three controlled shopping tests performed in randomly selected grocery stores by public accountants. Before many women were hired by public accounting firms, when three men with suits, ties and hats entered a grocery store on a Monday morning to begin the tests, everybody in the store thought the jig was up! In the controlled tests, the number of items, the cash tender and the change back was the same. The only difference was one test had no coupons, one had one and the other one had three coupons. All three shoppers went through the same check stand and cashier. Each shopper had a concealed stop watch. The second shopper timed the first, the third shopper timed the second, and the first shopper, loitering, timed the third. The additional time to process the orders containing coupons was costed out at the average cashiers salary and included in the coupon handling cost. Additional components of the handling cost included bookkeeping time, sorting by manufacturer, billing and accounts receivable and the interest cost until reimbursement was received.

When video cameras became available in the early Eighties, they were substituted for controlled shopping tests to determine the extra time required to accept a coupon at checkout. This allowed for many more shopping tests while measuring actual transactions. This approach was also less expensive since using the controlled test approach, sometimes tests had to be scrapped because the cashier was interrupted for various reasons or closed down before checking out all three test shoppers, etc. Also , the accounting firm ended up with bags of groceries which were donated to charities.

Cost accounting studies have also been performed on many other areas. Examples include cost per seat mile flown on commercial airlines, cost of filling a prescription in a pharmacy, cost of processing a check, cost of preparing an invoice, and cost of processing a loan application.

Litigation Support and Expert Witnessing

Litigation often involves an accounting determination of damages or a loss. For example, if a factory or warehouse burns down or is somehow put out of business, there are really two kinds of loss. The first is a property or physical loss. The second is a loss of income or profits because of the interruption of normal business due to the fire or whatever that resulted in the closing of the facility. Companies often purchase "business interruption " insurance against this type of loss. The calculation of a loss due to disruption of the business is often done by accountants who then may be asked to testify on the accuracy and reasonableness of the calculation, if this kind of situation results in litigation.

Another opportunity for accountants involving litigation is to act as an expert witness based on their experience and industry competence that they may have gained through years of working in a particular industry. They can testify as to typical expense ratios, margins or Income potential. Testimony could also include pricing arrangements, viability of a particular business in its industry, management compensation or compensation plans, causes of losses or bankruptcies and many other similar situations. Expert witnesses usually study relevant material, interview appropriate executives and employees, visit relevant facilities and perform other analysis they deem necessary. They may produce a written report and usually are subject to an exploratory deposition (a formal questioning by an attorney under oath which is recorded) prior to their actual testimony in court.

Industry Studies for Trade Associations

Very often, new developments in an industry require someone to take the lead and move the industry into a new phase. Accountants and consultants often work with leading industry trade associations to perform or facilitate studies to determine the costs and benefits of implementing new technology or new methods. Examples include the development and implementation of the Universal Product Code and product scanning at the checkout, implementation of Voluntary Interindustry Communication Standards, electronic payments, and coding of all medical invoices.

Accountants can offer impartial analysis of new technology or procedures and can make cost benefit calculations. They can then meet with industry groups to discuss results and make recommendations.

Industry Competence

Public accountants usually develop a comprehensive knowledge of the industry in which they work. This is generally called industry competence. Performing audits and a variety of special projects, gives them the opportunity, if not the necessity , to develop a detailed knowledge of the industry. This includes its operations, economics, terminology, organizational structure and risks and rewards.

Industry competence provides the accountant the opportunity to become a consultant to the industry, which opens up a wide variety of opportunities. This also can provide the accountant with career challenges over and above accounting. Working side by side with industry leaders, the accountant can be a valuable resource in helping to solve industry problems and challenges.

CHAPTER EIGHT

What Does a Chief Financial Officer (CFO) Do?

The Chief Financial Officer is one of the most important positions in any company. He or she is usually elected by the Board of Directors -- designated as Vice-President Finance or Senior Vice President and Chief Financial Officer. The CFO usually is a Certified Public Accountant, often with a masters degree. He or she may have had some experience in public accounting and may also have extensive experience in the industry as well as with the company for which he or she works. The CFO may also be a member of the Board of Directors.

Starting A Career in Accounting

When new hires initially start their careers, they are usually assigned to one aspect of the array of accounting areas. For example, this could be cash, which involves reconciling cash transactions each month from the bank statement to the accounting records. Or it could be accounts receivable, which involves determining collectability, reconciling payment or billing differences or discrepancies. This would also involve determination of the reserve for bad debts to make sure that the receivables are stated at net realizable value.

They may also be involved in checking inventories by observing the company's physical inventory and making and recording test counts to verify its accuracy. Thy may also make tests to determine if any obsolescence exists.

In summary, beginning accountants usually work on some specific area of accounting. Over time however, they usually are rotated to different areas, so that they are always learning something new.

After some initial period, accountants are usually promoted to a supervisory level which may be designated controller In private industry (as opposed to public accounting.) The highest accounting position that can be achieved in private industry is chief financial officer (CFO). Accountants can follow similar paths in not-for-profits or governmental bodies.

In today's complex business world many CFOs, because of their knowledge of the industry, are promoted to the CEO of the company, which is the highest level an officer can achieve. Following is a description of the various responsibilities and duties of the CFO.

Accounting and Reporting

The CFO's primary responsibility is to supervise the accounting and reporting of the company. In smaller companies, the CFO may directly perform selected accounting functions. In larger companies, these functions may be delegated to controllers and assistant controllers who have responsibility for various accounting and reporting areas. The record-keeping functions are usually maintained on computer-based systems.

The reporting function would include preparation of internal financial statements, usually on a monthly basis, which are provided to various levels of management so they can assess the results of operations. The CFO may distribute the statements along with a brief memo explaining results of operations, discussing variations from budget and other significant issues. There may also be a monthly management meeting where the CEO, other key management personnel and the CFO meet to review and discuss the results of operations.

For public companies(those whose stock is listed on a stock exchange) the SEC requires quarterly (10Q) and annual (10K) financial reports which are the responsibility of the CFO.

With regard to the preparation of financial statements and related disclosures, management and the CFO have the ultimate responsibility for their accuracy. He or she must make sure their supporting cast of controllers and assistance controllers are very capable of doing their job. He or she must make sure checks and balances and internal controls are in place to prevent errors or fraud. He or she must have enough knowledge of the industry and its operation, so that by simply reviewing the operating results and financial condition of the company, he or she can spot errors or out of line numbers, or at least make investigations so that unusual performance is justified by the underlying facts. Financial statements simply must be accurate.

The CFO is also responsible for working with the auditors as they plan and perform the annual audit of the company. The CFO needs to keep the auditors informed of any major changes in operations, or major financial transactions. Auditors would discuss any proposed adjustments to the financial statements with the CFO. The CFO would then have to agree or disagree with the proposed adjustments, and if required, make the adjustments to the financial statements before releasing them.

The CFO also works closely with the company's internal auditors. While they should be independent of the CFOs operation, they need to liaise together to discuss areas to be audited, to assess the results of the audits, and to take corrective action where required.

Budgets

In most companies, preparation of the annual budget is an important function. The CFO usually has the responsibility for the preparation of the annual budget. Budget worksheets are prepared under his or her supervision. These worksheets may show current year results to date, an estimate of the transactions for the remaining months, an estimated result for the year and the current year budget. A blank column is left for the next year's budget.

The worksheets are distributed to the various levels of the organization who initially prepare the next year's budget. This exercise is known as "budgeting from the ground up." The CFO then gathers all the completed worksheets and has them accumulated to get aggregate budgeted results. The budget is then reviewed with top management by the CFO. If unsatisfactory, it is sent down the line again, and various operating plans or assumptions are changed, until a satisfactory budget is achieved.

Internal Control

Internal controls are extremely important and are also the responsibility of the CFO. The function of internal control is to assure that the company has various procedures in place to provide reasonable assurance that the financial statements provided to management, the shareholders (either public or private) are accurate and are not materially misstated. Both the CEO and the CFO (the CAO if the CFO is not a CPA)have to sign a report which is included with public companies financial statements that the financial statements are reasonable accurate and that appropriate internal controls exist to reasonably assure that the process to prepare those statements is effective. The auditors of public companies, pursuant to the Sarbanes-Oxley Act, also have to audit the company's internal controls and issue a written opinion on them in their report to shareholders

It is also a function of internal control to protect the assets of the entity from misuse or theft or any other disposition not in accordance with managements or the Board of Directors directives.

Cash Management and Capital Needs

The CFO is responsible to make sure the company always has sufficient cash to fund its operations, make its payroll and pay its bills. Cash balances are usually monitored daily.

The CFO also has responsibility to assess the long-term capital needs of the company, and to recommend how these should be met. Should common stock be sold to the public, should the company issue some type of bonds, or should some facilities be mortgaged or leased. These are issues to be assessed by the CFO. Various alternatives should then be recommended to management. Cash flow schedules should also be prepared showing how these loans, if any, will be paid back. This is also the responsibility of the CFO, working with the CEO and others in top management..

Risk Assessment

The CFO may also be responsible to assess the various risks to the company. This could involve losses of assets due to fires or floods, liabilities the company may incur based on its operating facilities, products produced or sold or various business activities such as transportation, construction, providing healthcare, etc. The potential types of risks are dependent somewhat on the type of business the company is involved in.

Determination needs to be made whether these risks will be insured or self-insured. The CFO needs to work closely with the company's attorneys to determine how to assess and minimize various risks. Most companies have a variety of insurance policies to cover the company's major risks.

Cost Control and Reduction

The CFO is primarily responsible to watch and control costs. While cost control starts with the budget process, it needs to be monitored on an ongoing basis to make sure that no waste creeps into the operation, that expenses are adequately controlled, and that company personnel adhere to various company policies designed to control costs. Expense reports and various other expenses need to be closely monitored and approved by appropriate supervisory personnel. The ultimate responsibility is that of the CFO.

Tax Planning and Return Filings

The CFO is responsible to minimize taxes were possible, and file all required tax returns on a timely basis. While tax accountants may be directly responsible for this area, they usually report to the CFO, who oversees their work and determines various strategies to reduce the company's tax liability. Tax areas include federal and state income taxes, property taxes, sales taxes, and for global companies, international taxes and issues.

ERP and Other Systems

Most large companies have some type of Enterprise Resource Planning (ERP) systems. The systems generally include software that facilitates the record keeping and accounting for the company, as well as the financial reporting. It also integrates manufacturing, sales and service and customer relations.

All companies have "systems people", or outside consultants for this area. However, the CFO and his or her people are usually heavily involved in systems planning or changes or in installing new systems, because of the significant involvement with accounting and reporting. The CFO needs to determine that the financial reports are concise, meaningful, and provide adequate and understandable information to management so they can oversee the operation of the business effectively. He or she should also make sure that system support needs are met for all other areas of the company including production, operations, marketing, sales, human resources and research and development.

Mergers and Acquisitions

To the extent that a company gets involved in mergers and acquisitions, the CFO has a very significant role to play. He or she needs to review the financial statements of any target company, to determine if they are accurately stated and to discern the effectiveness of that company's operations. He or she also needs to determine how a merger or acquisition would fit with the company business and whether or not it would enhance his or her company's operation, particularly from a financial viewpoint.

He or she may have to prepare what is called pro forma financial statements which purport to show how the merger or acquired company would combine with his or her company. Pro forma financial statements usually involve various assumptions, which need to be made in detail to support the pro forma projections. The CFO needs to offer his unvarnished advice to the CEO regarding the merits of a planned merger or acquisition particularly from a financial viewpoint.

Other Attributes of the CFO

The CFO needs to be a good administrator. He or she needs to get along well with people, both within their department and in the organization in total. He or she needs industry competence and knowledge.

He or she has to have impeccable personal standards of integrity and honesty. He or she must stand up to anyone who tries to coerce or scare him or her into producing reports and financial statements he or she knows are false or are in error.

Many of the problems that occurred during the decade of the 1990's were caused because the CFO of the companies were pressured by various members of management to "make the numbers" so that stock prices would remain high or bonuses could be paid. These problems resulted in several large public companies falsifying financial statements. Once this unraveled, various investors and employees lost significant amounts of money and many lawsuits were initiated. Because of this, Congress passed the Sarbanes-Oxley Act in 2002 to put more pressure on both management and its auditor's to achieve a better result in terms of reporting financial results to the public.

The result has been that the position of the CFO in any company has been enhanced. However, there has been increased responsibility for the CFO to stand up to anyone who tries to coerce him or her into reporting inaccurate financial statements.

CHAPTER NINE

Personal Characteristics
Helpful for Accountants

Every profession has personal demands that should be considered by students, when deciding " if they would like to do that." Doctors. shouldn't be afraid of blood, race car drivers must like to speed, airline pilots shouldn't be afraid to fly, ship captains should love the sea, lawyers who litigate should love to argue and chefs should love to cook. But what about accountants?

First of all, accountants should be comfortable working with numbers. This means more than just using a calculator or computer. Ability to make calculations "in your head" helps. Examples are multiplication tables and division tables. They should also be good at solving word problems and have an acceptable knowledge of algebra.

Another good characteristic is skepticism like being a "doubting Thomas." Accountants shouldn't be gullible. Conclusions should be supported by the facts. Accountants also need to be very reliable. They can't be careless or flippant, can not "shoot from the hip." Accountants must have the right answer 100% of the time. If an accountant doesn't know, they shouldn't guess. Simply say "I don't know, but I'll find out."

Accountants should also refrain from always simply saying "no." They should try to be helpful. Think of a solution. As the saying goes, "there is more than one way to skin a cat." Be resourceful. Be creative. Be thoughtful. But always be right.

Importance of Honesty and Integrity

The most important characteristic of an accountant is honesty and integrity. They should never do anything they know is wrong. Numbers don't lie, so they shouldn't either. Accountants can become a most trusted advisor and should.

Accountants should avoid being cast as "green eye shade bookkeepers" with no personality. Accountants need to be able to get along with people. They need to be able to communicate in understandable terms. They should be viewed as leaders. They should be liked by their peers as well as by their reports. If they have something to say, they should not be afraid to speak up.

Accountants should be inquisitive. They should like to get the answer. They should develop habits that help them properly investigate issues so as to arrive at the correct answer. They should be intuitive, and have sound expectations based on knowledge of the industry in which they work.

Accountants should always be aware of better ways to do things. They should keep up with improvements in technology, changes in the business climate, and economic conditions and trends.

Ability to Write Well

Accountants should develop the ability to write well. They need to be able to communicate technical issues in non-technical language so other executives with different disciplines understand the issue being discussed by the accountant. They should be able to highlight issues succinctly and avoid endless trivia or details. Never mind how you got there, just explain what it is and why.

There is a difference between being an accountant in the private sector versus being an accountant in a public accounting firm. In the private sector, accountants may travel less and work out of this same office location for long periods of time.

Whereas an accountant in a public accounting firm, moves from client location to client location, which can involve more travel and more nights away from home. It takes a certain kind of personality not to mind constant change of venue that auditors generally must endure. Some accountants apprentice in public accounting firms when they're young and don't mind moving around. Then, as they mature, they take a job in private industry, which can provide a more stable work environment from a location standpoint.

Whatever profession one chooses, they should like what they do, like the work. If you really love what you do, work can be enjoyable or even fun. As the saying goes, "One person's work is another person's play."

CHAPTER TEN

Accounting by Industry

One of the most exciting and rewarding things about accounting is that the accountant must obtain extensive knowledge of the industry as well as the enterprise in that industry for which he or she works. Accountants must learn the operations of their company, the unique terminology that may be used, the organizational structure, as well as all the other aspects of the business, in order to do a proper job of accounting. Accountants tend to stay in the industry in which they started to work, particularly if they like that industry. Over the years the knowledge that an accountant gains from working in a particular industry gives that accountant an advantage and a feeling of comfort because they know how the industry works and what is expected of them as accountants

While the principles of accounting may be somewhat the same in each industry, based on GAAP. -- Generally Accepted Accounting Principles, the differences in what must be accounted for and how it's done, are quite variable. The concept of learning about an industry enough to be a good accountant, is called "industry competence." To rise to the top accounting position in a particular industry, the accountant must gain a fairly comprehensive understanding of the operations of that industry, and of his or her company.

Following is a sample listing of various industries for which accounting is generally unique;

>   -manufacturing
>   -food processing
>   -retailing
>   -wholesale distribution
>   -banking, finance
>   -insurance
>   -healthcare
>   -regulated industries or public utilities
>   -energy
>   -transportation
>   -movies and entertainment
>   -service industries
>   -real estate
>   -agriculture
>   -government

When viewing all these industries, it is amazing what the range of functions is, from manufacturing a car, packing a can of pineapple, operating a McDonald's restaurant, stocking spare parts for factories, making a loan, insuring a house or car, operating on a patient, drilling for oil, running a railroad, making a movie, playing in an orchestra, suing for damages, providing electricity to a group of homes, providing a hotel room, planting a corn crop or milking a cow, building a house or to running the government. Obviously a wide and disparate range of activities, but all must somehow be accounted for (keeping score.)

The good news is that every one of these industries needs accountants, whereas they all don't all need a scientist, a chemist, an architect, an engineer, a musician, an actor, a farmer, a teacher, a carpenter, a biologist, a doctor, or a chef, etc. While the goal of accounting is the same for each industry -- keeping score -- the methods and measurement techniques vary significantly.

To repeat, accountants need to understand how an industry works, it's terminology the economics and idiosyncrasies in order to do a proper job of accounting. Following is a brief discussion of the accounting nuances for some industries.

Manufacturing

While many products are manufactured outside the United States, the manufacturing industry in the US is still very significant. Automobiles, airplanes and many other products are manufactured in the U.S.

Manufacturing essentially involves converting raw materials into finished products. Other components involved in the manufacturing process include labor, machinery, factories, engineering, quality control, supplies, energy, etc. Raw materials consist of lumber, steel, other metals, plastics, wire, paper, etc. Manufacturing also involves purchasing subassemblies such as motors, molded plastics, prefabricated steel or metal etc.

One of the accounting challenges of the manufacturing industry is to determine the cost of product manufactured. Product costs include raw materials, labor and an allocation of the cost of the factory, commonly called overhead or factory burden. Often there is shrinkage or waste as the raw material is converted to the finished product. This loss must appropriately be accounted for and included in the product cost.

There are generally two types of labor in a manufacturing facility -- direct labor and indirect labor. Direct Labor is the term for the factory workers who are directly involved in the manufacture of the product.

They usually operate machinery used in the manufacturing process. They are sometimes involved in assembly of manufactured parts or subassemblies.

Indirect labor is involved in the operation of the factory or manufacturing facility, not directly related to making the product. This would include functions such as receiving, shipping, quality control, janitorial, supervision, accounting, and factory maintenance. These labor costs are included in factory overhead and allocated to the product cost on some overall basis such as number of items produced divided into the total cost of factory burden for a specified period.

Standard Costs

Accounting systems used to measure and control product cost, employ a concept called standard costs or a standard cost system. Standard costs are based or determined by testing or engineering. Standard Costs dictate how much raw material, direct labor, and factory overhead should be included in the cost of a product, based on the planned manufacturing process. Standard costs are usually developed each year, and may have to be adjusted from time to time if some of the cost components change drastically.

Once standard costs are in place, actual costs are compared to the standard costs to determine cost variances. Theoretically, variances should be small and balance out over time. However, large variances may indicate the factory is not operating efficiently or some cost components had cost increases since the standards were set. Accountants must analyze and determine why large variances occurred so corrective action can be taken, if required. Accountants performing this function must have a good knowledge of the plant operations and manufacturing processes. Accountants are also involved in the development of the standard costs, and this, then, helps them in the analysis of cost variances.

Variances are calculated for all three elements included in the standard costs – raw material, direct labor and factory overhead. Variances may only be significant in one or two elements of cost or in all three. Variances may be unfavorable or favorable. Unfavorable means more of that cost is being incurred than the standard allows. Favorable means the opposite, that less of a cost is being incurred than called for by the standard.

Raw material costs are affected by purchase price and the conversion process. If the price to purchase raw materials goes up, there will be unfavorable variances from standard. Also, if the quality of the material is poor, more of it may be used than the standard allowed thus creating an unfavorable variance.

Labor variances can occur if wage rates are increased or if poor quality material causes an increase in labor used. Changes in the manufacturing process can also cause labor to increase or decrease depending on what the change was.

Variances in factory burden can occur if any of the component costs change significantly or if the volume of units produced used for the allocation changes significantly. Reasons for variances must ultimately be determined, so corrective action can be taken, or standards can be updated.

Food and Related Products Processing

Food processing is a special type of manufacturing, with greater emphasis on the basic ingredients, as well as marketing of the finished products. Companies in this industry are known as consumer packaged goods or CPG companies. Processed foods generally include canned fruits and vegetables, sauces and juices, condiments, coffee and tea, sugar, flour and other ingredients, cereals, rice and stuffing, jams and jellies, etc.

Other items that are produced include processed meats and fish, dairy items including milk, milk byproducts, cheeses and ice cream. The emphasis is on the quality of the ingredients as well as on the attractiveness of the packaging.

Production plants must generally be concerned with sanitation and comprehensive quality control so that products do not pose any health risk to consumers. Processing plants also include facilities to slaughter cattle, hogs, lambs, and chickens and turkeys. While each facility has the same objective, they're physically quite different. After slaughter, carcasses are usually shipped to other plants for further processing or to food stores.

Accounting functions include identifying and allocating costs, costing a finished product based on yields and waste. Selling prices may be based more on market forces than product costs, however.

Measuring yield from processing raw foods is very important in the food industry, as they can be quite variable depending upon the quality of the ingredients purchased and the efficiency of the processing operation. Standard costs are generally used similar to other manufacturing, to control operations. Ingredients are usually a greater portion of cost as most processing is done by machines, reducing direct labor costs. Product quality and yield are closely monitored.

Some foods are sold fresh, and processing only includes culling bad items, and some limited packaging. This includes fresh fruits and vegetables and fresh fish.. Fresh meats may be cut from wholesale cuts to retail cuts and packaged in central distribution facilities or in meat departments in grocery and other retail stores.

Nonfood items also produced by CPG companies include paper and tissue products, soaps and detergents, bags, foil and kitchen and bathroom supplies. Sodas, water and juices are produced in bottling plants.

Health and beauty aids such as toothpaste, shampoo, cosmetics, shaving items and patent medicines are also items produced by CPG companies

CPG companies also spend a significant portion of their sales on trade promotions, trade relations and consumer advertising. They generally sell their products to retailers. However, they create a market for their products with consumers by advertising their products on TV, and in other media such as magazines, newspapers and the internet. They also issue coupons via FSI's (Free Standing Inserts) in Sunday papers, direct mail and the Internet.

Trade promotion occurs when consumer packaged goods companies, offer discounts to retailers or wholesalers in consideration of specific in-store marketing efforts, such as special displays, or lower prices, or for purchasing larger quantities than normal for a particular item. Food processors may also participate in industry conventions of retailers by sponsoring speakers, workshops, dinners or entertainment.

These various promotions are offered to retailers and wholesalers in a variety of ways. Allowances or discounts may be deducted off the invoice. In other cases, the retailer may bill-back the manufacturer, based on actual units sold. Retailers process coupons received from customers at the checkout and send them to clearinghouses who pay the retailer and then bill the issuing manufacturer. Retailers sometimes deduct these owed discounts or allowances from the manufacturer's invoice, giving rise to a large number of billing and paying discrepancies (deductions) which must ultimately be reconciled by accountants

Retailing Industry

Retailing involves the sale of finished goods or products to the ultimate consumer. The industry includes all types of retail stores including grocery stores, department stores, specialty stores, drug stores, discount stores, restaurants, mail-order via catalogs, online or Internet sales, and direct selling, either door-to-door or party plan.

The functions of the industry include purchasing, logistics of distribution, product display, marketing, advertising and selling. Sales include the selling price of the item, less markdowns or discounts. Costs include the purchase price of the product, labor, occupancy, supplies and overhead costs.

Accounting for this industry is directed to controlling the point-of-sale transaction so as to accurately record sales and account for and control the cash and other forms of payment received from the customer, such as debit or credit cards, checks, coupons, food stamps and gift cards. Retail stores may have many points of sale or places where customers can check out. Control is very important particularly since many sales are for cash. Control is accomplished by cash and sales reports completed at the point-of-sale based on the register controlling the transactions. These reports are audited by sales audit personnel.

Gross margin in this industry is calculated as a percentage of sales. For example, an item purchased for $6.00 that is sold for $10.00 said to have a 40% gross margin. This is also referred to as the markup percent. Inventories and sales are sometimes accounted for at retail and price reductions or markdowns are recorded and accumulated to determine the reduction in gross margin. This system is generally referred to as the "retail inventory method."

The critical numbers to be reported include sales increases or decreases, and gross margin percentages. All retailers are always concerned about sales. So the measurement or accounting for sales in a variety of ways is very important to the management of retailers. The overall measurement of the success or lack thereof for a retailer or retail store chain, is what is happening to sales at stores open at least 12 months, which is generally referred to as" same-store sales." If same-store sales are increasing, the conclusion is the retailer is doing very well. If they are decreasing, the opposite is assumed.

In addition, key productivity statistics, generally called KPIs -- Key Performance Indicators -- are also calculated for each retail store or department. Examples of these are as follows;

-sales per manhour (employee hours worked)
-sales per square foot of selling space
-amount of sale per customer transaction
-inventory shortage percent to sales
-mark down percent to sales
-labor cost percent to sales
-inventory turnover (cost of sales divided by average inventory)

Wholesalers

Wholesalers, also known as distributors, generally purchase various products from manufacturers, hold them in stock, and sell them to retailers, manufacturing plants, farmers, breweries, food processors, service organizations, etc. According to Naw (National Association of Wholesalers.) there are over 80 different commodity line wholesalers, many of whom have exclusive authorization for specific product lines of manufacturers. Examples are plumbing and heating, hardware, food, electrical, beer, sporting goods, marine, school supplies, pool and spa, foodservice, chemical, containers, floor coverings, wine and spirits, nursery and landscapers, etc.

Wholesalers take orders and deliver product to their customers' location on a timely basis. They must have sophisticated billing and inventory systems. Their customers rely on them for products needed to operate the businesses or plants. Wholesalers must maintain high in-stock positions so orders can be filled at a high service level, meaning out-of-stocks are 3% or less of sales orders.

They're essentially a warehouse operation. Some wholesalers also perform value added services, such as producing custom cut conveyor belts to fit a specific conveyor system in a customer's warehouse or factory. Another example would be repackaging manufacturer quantities to consumer marketable quantities.

Margins are low in the wholesale business, so expenses must be tightly controlled. Accountants must also pay particular attention to receivable collections to make sure customers stay current with their bills.

Banks and Finance Companies

This industry is much different than traditional manufacturing or distribution industries. Their operation involves handling cash and cash equivalents, initially as deposits for customers' accounts or investments, and then as loans and mortgages granted to customers who need financing.

Their income statements consist of interest income and service fees and their expenses are interest payments and administrative expenses. Banks also issue credit and debit cards and make income on the fees charged on transactions involving those cards.

Accountants need to carefully monitor interest rates as banks earn profits on interest rate spreads, or the difference between interest earned on loans and mortgages compared to interest paid to customers on deposits, certificates of deposits, etc. Accountants must also carefully monitor delinquencies and losses on loans and mortgages to make sure they remain within normal ranges.

Key performance indicators for banks include the following;

-Return on average assets
-Return on average equity
-Net interest margin
-Non-interest expenses/Assets
-Non-interest income/Assets
-Allowance for loan losses/Loans
-Efficiency ratio (interest margin, plus other income/ non-interest expence)
-Loan/Deposit ratio
-Capital/ Assets

Insurance Industry

The insurance industry includes casualty insurers, life insurers, liability insurers, workers compensation, and specialty insurance. The insurance industry also includes insurance brokers and agents who sell insurance to the public and to businesses.

Insurance company revenue includes premiums received, miscellaneous revenue and interest and dividends on investments. Expenses include claims paid and reserves for future claims, commissions to agents and brokers and administrative expenses.

The accounting challenge is to make sure reserves for claim losses are adequate to cover anticipated claims. This is usually based on historical analysis of claims experience, adjusted for anticipated changes in the market place. In addition, insurances companies employ actuaries who calculate required reserves for claim losses.

Healthcare Industry

The healthcare industry consists of doctors, dentists, therapists, nurses, hospitals, clinics, laboratories and nursing homes. The industry is somewhat unique because it operates as a three-legged stool with patients, providers and payers all separate entities. Patients receive services from doctors and hospitals (the providers), but payment is made by third-party payers, such as insurance companies, corporate or business benefit plans, union plans, Medicare and Medicaid.

All billing for services provided must be properly supported and coded with Medical Billing Codes, such as procedure codes which are very detailed and somewhat cumbersome to apply to billings. This system has resulted in providers being paid for services rather slowly, as the billings work their way through the cumbersome system.

Hospitals also provide a certain amount of "free care" to indigent patients. Hospitals attempt to cover the cost of these services from other revenue.

Productivity records include bed utilization rates in hospitals, readmissions relative to initial treatments, infection rates, complication rates etc. Some hospitals join with various hospital groups to compare their operating ratios with those in the group. This information is then used to improve the services provided to patients.

Hospitals and other healthcare providers also maintain detailed patient records of patient visits, treatments, symptoms, results, etc. these have traditionally been manual, but efforts are now being made to convert and prepare them in electronic format. Any savings are not as great as initially estimated. However, it is believed that this will help doctors and others more readily and effectively treat patients in need of care.

Regulated Industries

Regulated Industries also sometimes referred to as Public utilities consist of electric companies, natural gas companies, and water companies. They formerly included telephone companies, but these companies have now been deregulated. Rates charged by public utilities are governed by the states Public Utility Commissions. Rates are generally based on the cost of service, plus a fair rate of return to the company.

Because of this method of regulation, public utilities maintain very detailed property cost records generally referred to as unit property records. These records are needed and are relied upon when the utilities requests rate increase, because production costs have increased.

Accountants often testify in the required rate hearings regarding requested rate increases. They are usually involved in the calculation of the cost increases that give rise to the basis of the rate increases. They usually testify on the reliability of the cost data being provided by the utility to justify the rate increase. Accountants often become frequently used expert witnesses in these matters.

Energy

The energy industry consists of companies that explore for oil and gas, mine coal, and refine crude oil into gasoline and other fuels. It also includes nuclear, wind, solar and ethanol. It also includes pipeline companies that transmit oil and gas, from production areas to refineries and consumption areas. It also includes companies that provide required equipment to these companies.

The cost structure for exploration companies is unique as it involves leases on land on which companies plan to drill, intangible as well as tangible drilling costs and dry holes. Intangible drilling costs include site preparation, wages, fuel, supplies, repairs and all other cost to prepare the well for drilling. Tangible costs include well piping, pumping and other equipment.

For tax purposes, oil companies are allowed to elect to write off 70% of intangible drilling costs in the year incurred with balance written off over 60 months.

There are two alternative accounting methods for oil and gas exploration companies. One is called the Successful Efforts method. This requires the company to capitalize (record as an asset) only those expenses associated with successful wells. Dry hole costs must be expensed as incurred.

The other method is the Full Cost method, where all operating costs related to drilling wells are capitalized, regardless of whether the wells are successful or not. Under each method, capitalized costs are written-off (charged to expense) as revenue is earned.

Transportation Industry

The transportation industry involves moving both people and things. It consists of airlines, trains, buses, trucks, barges and ships. The industry is generally very competitive. People are generally transported by planes, trains and ships and locally by buses or subway trains.

Products are moved by container ships, airplanes, trucks, and railroads. Container ship's move a significant amount of product from China and other countries where they are manufactured, to countries where they are consumed. Tankers also move crude oil from the Middle East to China, the US and other consuming countries.

Accountants must be concerned that rates charged are sufficient to cover costs. In the area of imports, customs and duties must also be adequately handled to assure smooth receipt and delivery of purchased goods. Risks must be assessed in terms of potential dollar losses, and adequate insurance must be maintained to cover these risks.

Accountants are also often involved in cost calculations such as cost per seat mile flown on airlines. These calculations help management compare their costs to their competitors or to determine pricing strategies.

Movies & Entertainment

In the movie industry, accountants have major roles to play particularly as movies are produced. They generally control and pay all costs associated with production, wherever it is being done. They pay all living and maintenance costs and various other costs associated with movie production.

Production accountants generally perform three functions;

> -bookkeeping and controlling petty cash which ranges much higher than in other industries
> -reporting actual costs compared to budgets usually on a weekly basis
> -auditing as sometimes funds can be misused. The production accountant must be vigilant to make sure all expenditures are appropriate and properly supported

Live entertainment events involve controlling ticket sales and expenses related to the cost of the entertainment..

Service Industries

Service industries include public accounting firms, consulting firms, law firms, architectural firms, engineering firms, advertising agencies, public relations firms and manpower outsourcing firms. These firms generally bill based on hours charged or spent on the job. Billing rates must be adequate to cover applicable salaries and fringe benefits, as well as "downtime", training and other non-billable time. Lawyers sometimes perform services on a contingent fee arrangement, usually as a percentage of an award received by the party they represented. Advertising agencies may bill based on a percentage of the cost of the ads placed.

Key performance indicators are percent of chargeable time to total available time per person and per engagement. These statistics are also maintained by office, and by operating division within the office.

Another key statistic is write- offs (time not billed) per job or as percentage of billable time. Most jobs have some write-offs for inefficiencies, research, etc. but write-offs must be within a tolerable range so that the organization can be profitable.

Real Estate

The real estate industry consists of constructing homes, factories or buildings. It also includes sales of existing properties by real estate agents. Many properties are also leased by various companies and agents who function as leasing representatives.

During construction, accountants must carefully control costs. Sub-contracting should be based on detailed bids. Waivers of lien should be obtained when sub contractors are paid.

When companies lease office buildings or factories, accountants should carefully read and study the lease to make sure the agreed space and rental costs are accurately portrayed. Leasehold allowances should be adequately explained. Renewal options should be considered and the details should be reviewed.

Agriculture

Farming may be categorized into two main components -- raising crops or tending orchards and raising animals for byproducts such as milk or for slaughter for meat. In both types of farming, extensive acres of land are involved. In an accounting sense, land is never depreciated, because it exists indefinitely. Therefore, while the cost is part of the investment required for farming, its cost is not included in the income and expense calculations, unless it is leased.

For crop farming which includes grains and various vegetables, the cost would include seeds, fertilizer, herbicides, insecticides. Also included, would be depreciation on farming equipment, labor, and taxes and insurance. Similar costs would be incurred for tending orchards.

Farm animals give rise to different accounting issues. Dairy cows are more or less like permanent assets. They are fed and cared for and give milk over approximately a 20 year period. They calf every year (or are supposed to.) Female calves are added to the herd, while male calves are usually sold for veal or to cow calf ranchers. Dairy farmers, usually have pasture land for grazing, and they grow corn to feed the herd, as a supplement and in winter..

Costs for a dairy operation include equipment depreciation, veterinary services, feed, building depreciation and maintenance. The initial cost of the herd, if purchased, would be depreciated over the estimated life of the cows. Off-springs have no "cost" other than maintenance.

Beef herds are usually called "cow calf" operations. Some ranchers sell calfs to feed lots for maturation, while others raise them for slaughter. Breed cows need to calf each year for the operation to be effective. Ranchers generally raise their animals on pasture land, but may supplement their feed, particularly in winter.

Similar operations apply to pigs, sheep and lambs, and poultry. Flocks of sheep may also be maintained for wool.

Government

Governments includes the federal government, state governments, city and municipal governments, such as towns, counties, and separate agencies. Government accounting is usually on a partial accrual basis, and may not recognize in its primary financial statements all liabilities or assets.

CHAPTER ELEVEN

Entity Formats and Sources of Capital

Business organizations as well as other enterprises such as not-for- profits, adopt various legal forms or types of entities to house their operations. These various entities also provide vehicles by which the capital required to support the operations can be raised. This chapter discusses several of these types of legal entities and the methods by which they afford businesses the ability to raise capital.

Sole Proprietorships

The simplest and most basic form of business enterprise is the sole proprietorship. This is simply a business venture operated by an individual under his or her own name or using a DBA -- i.e. Doing Business As -- an assumed name. Examples are Bob Jones and Associates, or Mrs. Smith's cookies. In other words, an individual simply starts a business with no separate legal entity. The business transactions are kept separate from the person's personal finances. The sole proprietor may work out of his or her home, or may own or rent a separate physical facility. A separate set of records is maintained to keep track of the business operations and to determine profit or loss. To obtain a legal DBA, usually requires it to be registered. The sole proprietor may hire employees and put them on an official payroll. Often trades people, such as plumbers, electricians, carpenters, or handymen or professionals such as accountants, lawyers or doctors operate as sole proprietors.

Sources of capital for a sole proprietorship may be provided from savings of the sole proprietor, or from a mortgage or home equity loan on the sole proprietor's residence, or from a bank or finance company loan. Funds could also be provided by friends or relatives.

One of the disadvantages of a sole proprietorship is that any liabilities incurred by the business venture, can be assessed against the sole proprietor's other assets, such as an owned residence, stocks or bonds, etc. While insurance can be purchased to cover the risk, it can be very expensive, depending upon the likelihood of potential liabilities from the operation of the business.

From a tax standpoint, the income or loss of the sole proprietorship is included on the personal return of the sole proprietor. The operation of the business is included on schedule C. of the form 1040 federal income tax return. Any income or loss in the business accrues directly to the sole proprietor.

Partnership

A simple partnership is similar to a sole proprietorship, except two or more people are partners and owners of the business. The partnership may involve equal partners -- 50% each -- or unequal partners -- 60% versus 40% or 80% versus 20%, or multiple partners. A partnership is usually documented by a written partnership agreement. A separate set of accounting records is maintained to record the operations of the business. Any income or loss is distributed directly to the partners in accordance with the partnership agreement

The simple partnership does not protect the partners from any liability incurred by the business. They are personally liable and any personal assets are at risk. Insurance can be purchased to cover the risks, but it could be very expensive.

From an income tax viewpoint, a separate partnership tax return must be prepared on form 1065, and each partner's share of income or loss reported on a form K-1 and their share of income or loss is included on their personal tax return. Generally the partnership pays no taxes. Sources of capital would be the same as for a proprietorship.

Corporation

A corporation is a legal entity authorized by a state. Every state provides for "incorporation," but most publicly held corporations have been incorporated in the State of Delaware, because it's governing rules are generally favorable to a business. Corporations have common shares which represent the ownership, and it may also have preferred shares, a limited form of ownership. Preferred shares usually have a stated dividend rate, which must be paid from earnings before any earnings accrue to the common shareholders. After the preferred shareholders receive their dividends, all the remaining earnings accrue to the common shareholders. Corporations have authorized and issued shares. Authorized shares are designated when the corporation is set up. Shares are issued when they are paid for by the shareholders. Shares may be designated as par or no par value. Par value states a fixed dollar amount per share -- say, $100 per share. This means that persons who own the shares paid into the corporation at least $100 per share No par shares mean that a stated or agreed amount has been paid for the shares, but no specific amount is attached to the shares as a par value. The amount paid for the shares provide initial operating capital for the business.

A corporation is a separate legal person under the law, and it can continue in perpetuity if properly maintained and setup. The liabilities incurred by the corporation can only be paid from corporate assets. The shareholders and officers cannot be held personally liable for the liabilities of the corporation, unless they commit fraud or otherwise misuse the assets of the corporation.

The corporation is taxed as a separate entity and must pay tax on its net income. Shareholders can receive net income earned when the corporation declares and pays dividends. Dividends are then taxed again to the shareholders. In certain instances, if a corporation has less than 100 shareholders, it can elect to be treated as a partnership via electing what is called Subchapter S status. This avoids any corporate tax, and the income whether distributed or not is included in the taxable income of the shareholders, in proportion to their shares.

The corporate structure is also available for a not-for-profit organization. In this case, the corporation has no shares or shareholders, but has members and member equity. Not-for-profit corporations by their very nature are not required to pay income tax.

Limited Liability Company

A Limited Liability Company (LLC) is a cross between a partnership and a corporation. Generally, the liabilities of the company cannot be assessed against the owners of the LLC. There could be one owner or multiple owners. The income is treated as though the company was a partnership, and is passed through to the owners and included on their personal tax returns so the LLC pays no income tax.

Sources of capital for an LLC are similar to those of a proprietorship or a partnership.

Limited Liability Partnership

A Limited Liability Partnership(LLP) is a partnership in which the partners have limited liability,. Each partner may be responsible for their own actions, but they are not liable for the actions or negligence of the other partners. Limited Liability Partnerships are organized under state laws. Most states provide for LLP organizations.

Often, professional organizations such as public accounting firms, law firms, architectural firms and consulting firms are organized as LLP's.

Initial capital is provided by the partners, who may finance the capital contribution from personal bank loans or from personal assets. LLP's pay no income tax as their income is included in the personal returns of its partners in proportion to their partnership interests.

Master Limited Partnership

A Master Limited Partnership (MLP) is a limited partnership that is publicly traded on a stock exchange. These limited partnerships have a general partner who usually operates the partnership. These partnerships must obtain 90% of their income from activities associated with the production, development or transmission of oil, gas or coal.

Because they are partnerships, they avoid corporate income taxes. Their income is distributed to the limited partners, who must include it in their personal tax returns.

Capital is raised from the partnership interests that are sold on various stock exchanges and from loans from banks or other commercial lenders. Initial investment capital may be provided by the organizing partners.

Real Estate Investment Trusts (REITs)

Real Estate Investment Trusts, commonly called REITs, are corporate entities investing in real estate, mortgages or building leases. This allows them to avoid paying any income tax, as long as they pay out at least 90% of their income to their investors. REIT's generally operate, lease or finance commercial real estate such as offices, warehouses, apartments, shopping centers, hotels and hospitals.

REITs may be publicly traded or privately held. Capital is provided from the sale of securities, private investment funds or mortgages.

CHAPTER TWELVE

Rule Making Bodies and Their Functions

Accounting, auditing, financial reporting and tax planning and return preparation are governed by five major organizations as well as by various legislative initiatives passed by the U.S. Congress. Not every aspect of the profession is regulated by the governing bodies, generally accepted accounting principles have evolved from various sources over a long period of time. Much of what is dealt with by these organizations is in response to current or timely economic events and various business trends.

The five major organizations are as follows;

- -Financial Accounting Standards Board -- FASB
- -Public Company Accounting Oversight Board -PCAOB
- -Committee of Sponsoring Organizations of the Treadway Commission COSO
- -Securities and Exchange Commission -- SEC
- -Internal Revenue Service -- IRS

The functions of each of these organizations is briefly discussed as follows.

Financial Accounting Standards Board FASB

The FASB was established in 1973 replacing the Committee on Accounting Procedure (CAP) and the Accounting Principles Board (APB,) which was an organization sponsored by the American Institute of Certified Public Accountants (AICPA). The FASB is a private not-for-profit organization, whose members are selected by the Financial Accounting Foundation (FAF) and whose operating cost is also funded by the FAF. The members must be truly independent by severing relationships with all other organizations.

The mission of the FASB is " to establish and improve the standards of financial accounting and reporting for the guidance and education of the public, including issuers, auditors and users of financial statements." Prior rulings of the APB remain in force unless modified or changed by the FASB.

Public Company Accounting Oversight Board PCAOB

The PCAOB was created by the Sarbanes-Oxley act which was passed by Congress in 2002 in response to some significant misstatements of financial statements of public companies. The PCAOB is a privately held not-for-profit company. The functions of the PCAOB are as follows

-register public accounting firms that audit public companies
-set audit, independence and other standards for public companies
-conduct audits of public accounting firms and take disciplinary action, if required

-regulate the non-audit services that may be offered by public accounting firms to audit clients

The SEC has the power to appoint and remove Board members, to approve its budget, and to hear appeals of PCAOB disciplinary reports.

Committee of Sponsoring Organizations of the Treadway Commission COSO

COSO was formed in 1985 as a result of a commission headed by James Treadway, a former SEC Commissioner, which focused on improving internal controls and strengthening the reliability of financial reporting as well as compliance with laws and regulations. COSO is supported by five organizations including the Institute of Management Accountants (IMA), the American Accounting Association(AAA), the American Institute of Certified Public Accountants (AICPA) the Institute of Internal Auditors (IIA) and the Financial Executives International (FEI.)

The COSO framework focuses on defining internal control, risk assessment, control activities, information and communication and monitoring. The ultimate objective is for companies to maintain consistent internal controls to assure as much as possible that the financial reporting is reasonable accurate and that entity assets are used only for entity purposes and not in any way misapplied or misused.

Securities and Exchange Commission SEC

The Securities and Exchange Commission was created in 1934 by act of the United States Congress. The main function of the SEC as it relates to accounting and financial reporting is to regulate the issuance of financial statements of public companies. The frequency, format and information to be included in the financial reports is the purview of the SEC. As to GAAP, the SEC has generally demurred to the accounting profession for the development and codification of Generally Accepted Accounting Principles.

Internal Revenue Service IRS

While the Congress of the United States passes legislation regarding income taxes, the detailed regulations implementing the laws are written by the IRS. Accountants need to maintain records that facilitate the preparation of required tax returns. Often the reporting of revenue and expense for tax purposes may be different than for book or reporting purposes to shareholders.

Appendix One

XYZ Company, Inc

This fictitious company is included to better illustrate the mechanics, concepts and reports of accounting and auditing. The name of the company is XYZ Company, Inc.

The company manufactures and sells personal computers and printers, tablets and cell phones. It also has an extensive consulting practice. Most of the manufacturing is done in China and Japan, but the company has one manufacturing facility in Houston, Texas.

The county's annual revenues are approximately $1 billion consisting of $400 million in computer and printer sales $100 million in tablet sales $200 million in cell phone sales and over $300 million in consulting. The company is relatively small compared to its rivals. Also it is relatively new beginning operations in 2002, and is considered a niche player.

The company has over 1200 employees, with over 600 involved in consulting, 150 in sales and marketing, 125 involved in manufacturing and warehousing, and over 300 involved in management, administration and accounting. The company's headquarters are in Houston, where it also has a manufacturing facility and a distribution warehouse.

Distribution warehouses are also located in Long Beach, California, St. Louis, Missouri, Atlanta, Georgia, and Newark, New Jersey. The company also has a research and development lab at its headquarters in Houston, Texas.

The company sells its products to chain retailers and independents. The company also sell some products over the Internet. Products manufactured in Asia are received in Long Beach from container ships and are transported to a distribution warehouses via common carrier.

The company is owned by several major investors, and some members of top management. Certain key employees also have stock options.

Appendix Two

Chart of Accounts – XYZ Company, Inc

Assets	100's
Current Liabilities	300's
Long Term Debt	400.s
Shareholders Equity	500's
Revenues	600's
Costs of Sales	700's
Expenses	800's
Interest Expense	900's
Suffixes	
Corporate	-00
Houston	-01
Long Beach	-02
St. Louis	-03
Atlanta	-04
Newark	-05

All of the accounts below would have one or multiple suffixes. Each account with a suffix is a separate account. For example, 100-00 and 100-01 are two separate accounts.

Cash	100
Marketable Securities	105
Accounts Receivable – Computers & Printers	110
Accounts Receivable-Tablets	111
Accounts Receivable-Cell Phones	112
Accounts Receivable= Consulting	113
Inventory- Computers	120
Inventory-Printers	121
Inventory-Tablets	122
Inventory-Cell Phones	123
Prepaid Expenses	130
Supplies	135
Prepaid taxes	140
Land	150
Plant	151
Reserve for Depreciation-plant	161
Equipment	152
Reserve for depreciation-equipment	162
Delivery vehicles	153
Reserve for depreciation-delivery vehicles	163
Patents and copyrights	175
Reserve for amortization –patents & copyrights	185
Accounts Payable	300
Accrued expenses	301
Reserve for Income Taxes	302
Current maturities of Long term debt	350

Bank Loans	400
Subordinated debentures	405
Deferred Income Taxes	450
Other liabilities	460
Common Stock	500
Paid-In Capital	510
Retained Earnings	520
Sales-Computers	600
Sales-Printers	605
Sales-Tablets	610
Sales-Cell Phones	615
Consulting Revenue	620
Financing Income	650
Cost of sales-Computers	700
Cost of Sales-Printers	705
Cost of Sales-Tablets	710
Cost of Sales-Cell Phones	715
Cost of Sales-Consulting	720
Financing Expense	750
Plant payroll	800
Selling Payroll	805
Consulting Payroll	810
Administrative payroll	815
Payroll taxes	830
Medical Benefits	835
Workman's Compensation	840
Travel Expenses	845
Advertising	850
Depreciation	855
Amortization	860
Insurance	865

Professional Services   870
Utilities   875
Research and Development   880

Interest Expense   900

Appendix Three

Accounting and Financial Definitions

Accounting

The discpline of maintaining a set of records where financial transactions are recorded and used to prepare financial reports

Audit

The act of examining using agreed upon standards a financial statement, function or entity to determine its accuracy, validity or truthfulness.

Balance Sheet

Financial statement listing all assets and deducting all liabilities of an entity resulting in the determination of a net surplus or a net deficit as of a given date.

Bond

A formal document representing borrowing by a corporation or a government with a set rate of interest, sometimes secured by specific assets of the entity issuing the bonds and with a specific maturity date.

Corporation	A legal entity created pursuant to the laws of a state which exists in perpetuity and is owned by its shareholders or in the case of not-for-profits not owned by anybody but controlled by its Board of directors or by members
Credit	Accounting term for an entry to increase a liability or revenue account or to decrease an asset,expense or cost account. Also, an increase in a bank account or a monetary amount granted to an individual or entity reducing amounts owed.
Common stock	Shares of a corporation representing its ownership
Convertible bonds	Bonds granting the holders the right at some time to exchange the bonds for common stock in the issuing corporation based on a predetermined price per share.
Callable bonds	Bonds which may be redeemed (paid off) before their stated maturity date by the issuer based on stated dates, after which they may be called for redemption.
Certificate of Deposit	A form of investment issued by a bank for a fixed period and at a set rate of interest and guaranteed by the FDIC up to $250,000
Checking account	Bank account on which the owner writes paper checks, makes deposits, or allows direct deposits and/or direct payments (debits) or conducts online banking.

CEO | Chief Executive Officer of a corporation or other entity. Highest ranking officer of the corporation or entity.

CFO | Chief Financial Officer of a corporation or entity in charge of all accounting and financial areas of the corporation or entity.

Debit | Accounting term for an entry to increase an asset or cost or expense account or to decrease a revenue or liability account. Also, a bank charge to an account.

Debenture bonds | Corporate borrowing represented by formal documents not specifically secured by particular corporate assets, but payable from the overall assets if the corporation, having a stated rate of interest and a specific maturity date.

ERP systems | Enterprise Resource Planning systems integrating all accounting, reporting, administrative and operating functions of an enterprise, supported by comprehensive software.

External Financial Statements | Financial statements prepared for the public including shareholders, investors, analysts and the SEC.

Fiscal Year | The 12 months designated as the period to be accounted for by the financial reports. It can be any consecutive 12 month period including the calendar year

General Ledger   Basic accounting record where all transaction of an entity are ultimately entered and accumulated.

Government bonds   Bonds issued by the federal government.

Historical cost   Original purchase price in dollars of items bought including land, buildings and equipment.

Imprest account   Bank account with a fixed balance amount. Payments out are timely reimbursed to maintain the fixed balance.

Income statement   Financial statement listing all revenues and deducting all costs and expenses for a set period of time to determine a profit or loss. Also called a profit and loss statement or simply an earnings statement.

Industry competence   Term used to describe knowledge a person has of a given industry's operations, economics and terminology.

Internal audit   Function of a company or entity in which its accounting and operating procedures, assets and liabilities are subject to audit checks by a separate department of the entity or by an outside organization to whom the process has been outsourced.

Internal control   The procedures in place in a corporation or other entity to assure that the preparation of

	its financial statements results in reasonable accuracy and to safeguard its assets.
Internal financial Statements	Financial statements prepared for use only by management personnel of the entity
Inventory turnover	A calculation made by dividing average inventory into annual cost of sales
Journal	In an accounting sense, initial records where similar transactions are posted (recorded,) i.e. check register, payroll journal, etc.
LLC	Limited Liability Company set up pursuant to a state law, with some characteristics similar to a corporation (limited liability) and some similar to a partnership (owned by its partners.)
LLP	Limited Liability Partnership similar to an LLC, but generally used by accountants, lawyers or other professionals.
Not-for-Profit	Term used for entities such as schools, hospitals, charities, think tanks and others who are organized pursuant to not-for-profit laws of states and who pay no income tax and who are not owned by shareholders, but are controlled by a Board of Directors or by members.
Partnership	A legal entity formed pursuant to a legal agreement owned by two or more partners.

Preferred stock	Form of corporate ownership usually with no voting rights, with a fixed dividend amount per share and with a right to assets in liquidation ahead of the common shareholders.
Public Company	Company whose common or preferred shares or bonds are offered to the public including individuals, mutual funds, hedge funds and retirement and pension funds
Savings account	Account in a bank, savings and loan association, or credit union with a set rate of interest, but usually with no check writing privileges.
Subsidiary	Corporation whose outstanding shares are wholly or partially owned by another corporation.
Treasury bills	A form of investment issued by the federal government usually with short maturities – 4 weeks to 52 weeks-and purchased at a discount by the investor who receives face (stated) value at maturity.

Appendix Four

History of the Profession and its Major Accounting Firms

The study of the history of accounting firms provides the student with some historical background material which shows how the profession started and to where it has now evolved. Most accounting firms have English roots dating back to the 19th century. Accounting firms are primarily named after the accountants who started them. Most firms experienced several mergers resulting in name changes over the years.

During the latter half of the 20th century there was the "Big Eight" accounting firms. These firms ultimately merged and with the demise of one firm, the result is now the " Big Four" accounting firms. Following is a brief synopsis of the origin and significance of the history of these firms and the development and growth of the profession. (Much of the information is based on information listed in the bibliography.)

Events Fueling Growth of the Profession

The growth and relevance of the profession really occurred in the twentieth century. Prior to this time, while companies had accountants, their role was limited. In some cases, there was no formal determination of net income. The United States did not have an income tax until the twentieth century.

While many British firms were founded in the nineteenth century, their activities were mainly in the U. K. Most US firms and UK firms opened offices in the US near the end of the nineteenth century or the beginning of the twentieth century.

The events that fueled the growth of the profession include the following;

8. In 1896, New York passed a law that restricted the use of the title Certified Public Accountant to those who passed a state examination. Soon after, many states passed similar laws.
9. The rapid growth of industrialization increased the need for accountants and auditors.
10. In 1913, the Federal Reserve Board was established. The Federal Trade Commission was formed in 1914. Both of these new regulatory agencies led to the creation of standards and guidelines for independent public accountants.
11. In 1913, the US passed its first income tax on both corporations and individuals. This created the need for corporations to calculate their net income. It also, created the need for income tax expertise in the profession and its accounting firms.
12. In 1902, US Steel became the first US company to allow its shareholders to elect its outside auditors.
13. During the first World War, Arthur Young & Co. was hired by the British government to determine the cost of manufacturing Enfield rifles. It was one of the first firms to expand its services beyond audit.
14. In 1918, the Federal Reserve issued a pamphlet, "Approved Methods for the preparation of Balance Sheet Statements."

15. In 1930, Arthur Andersen (the man) acknowledged the significance of industry competence as he said no one can effectively provide audit and advisory services to all industries, but must limit their work to specific industries in which they have expertise.

16. The stock market crash of 1929 brought on the creation of the securities laws of 1933 and 1934, and the creation of the Securities and Exchange Commission in 1934. These laws created more work and opportunity for accountants.

17. In 1933, the New York Stock Exchange, required all listed companies to have audits by independent public accountants and also required them to follow certain standard accounting methods.

18. In 1943, Price Waterhouse began to actively recruit female college graduates for a special eleven week course at Northwestern University in accounting and auditing.

19. In the decade after the end of World War II, public accounting firms developed management consulting practices. Ernst & Ernst added a Management Services Division to provide services such as systems development and installation, operation research, and general management consulting.

20. In the 1950's, auditors began to leverage their audit experience to being able to examine or review the business as a whole. This allowed them to become trusted business advisors to management. Touche Ross recognized that the complexities of auditing could result in an undue emphasis on mechanics, so they wanted to develop thinking auditors and provided additional training to this end. This increased their appreciation of a companies internal controls and led to the development of the "integrated audit program."

Development and Origin of the "Big Eight"

Deloitte Haskin &Sells

In 1845 William Deloitte opened an office in London. Deloitte was the first company to be appointed auditor of a public company, the Great Western Railway. Deloitte opened an office in New York in 1880.

In 1896, Charles Waldo Haskins and Elijah Watt Sells formed Haskins & Sells in New York. It was the first major firm in the United States established by American rather than British accountants. They merged with Deloitte & Co. in 1952 to become Deloitte Haskins & Sells.

The Elijah Watt Sells award was created in 1923 by the American Institute of Certified Public Accountants to recognize outstanding performance in the uniform CPA examination. The award was developed to honor Elijah Watt Sells who was one of the first to become a CPA in New York and was active in helping create the American Institute of Certified Public Accountants –AICPA.

Touche Ross Bailey & Smart

In 1898, George Touche established an office in London. In 1900, he merged with John Niven to form Touche Niven in New York. In 1947, they merged with George Bailey a Detroit accountant and A. R. Smart to form Touche Niven Bailey & Smart. The firm grew rapidly in part by establishing a management consultant function. In 1960 after forming close links with the Canadian organization Ross and the British organization George R. Touche they were renamed Touche Ross Bailey & Smart.

Coopers &Lybrand

In 1854 William Cooper started an accounting firm in London, which became Cooper Brothers, when his three brothers joined the firm. In 1898, Robert Montgomery, William Lybrand, Adam Ross and his brother Edward Ross formed the firm of Lybrand, Ross Bros.& Montgomery in the United States.

Between 1950 and 1966, a significant number of British accounting firms merged into or were acquired by Cooper Brothers. In 1957, Cooper Brothers, Lybrand, Ross Bros.& Montgomery and a Canadian firm McDonald Currie & Co. agreed to adopt the name Coopers & Lybrand for their international practice. In 1973, all three firms agreed to change their name to Coopers & Lybrand.

Ernst &Whinney

The original firm was founded in 1849 in England as Harding and Pulletin. Frederick Whinney also joined the firm in 1849. When his sons also joined the firm, it was renamed Whinney Smith and Whinney in 1894.

In 1903, the firm of Ernst & Ernst was established in Cleveland by Alvin Ernst and his brother Theodore. In 1924, Ernst & Ernst allied with Whinney Smith and Whinney. In 1979, they formally merged to form the firm of Ernst and Whinney.

Arthur Young & Co.

In 1906, a Scotsman Arthur Young and his younger brother, founded Arthur Young & Co. in Chicago, ostensibly to handle the affairs of

British investment companies. In 1913, when the US first established an income tax, the firm establish a tax department.

In 1921, Arthur Young formed a national partnership of five offices with headquarters in New York. In 1957, Arthur Young & Co. was the first big eight accounting firm to elect a female partner.

Peat, Marwick Mitchell &Co

The firm was initially established in 1867 when William Barclay Peat founded an accounting firm in London. In 1897, James Marwick was a cofounder of Marwick, Mitchell & Co. in New York, just one year after the New York legislature created the designation Certified Public Accountant. In 1911, William Barclay Peat & Company merged with Marwick Mitchell & Co. to form Marwick Mitchell Peat & Co .In 1925 the name was changed to Peat Marwick Mitchell & Co.

Arthur Andersen & Co.

Arthur Andersen & Co. was formed in 1913 as Andersen Delaney & Co. by two former employees of Price Waterhouse & Co., Arthur Andersen and Clarence Delaney. In 1918, the name was changed to Arthur Andersen & Co. Arthur Andersen was also a professor at Northwestern University.

The firm grew rapidly by adhering to strict accounting principles even if it meant losing a client. In the 1930's the firm was engaged to audit the public utility holdings of Samuel Insull. As a result, the firm developed significant clients in this industry.

It also installed the first business computer in 1954 at General Electric. This was the beginning of a large systems consulting practice initially called Andersen Consulting and now named Accenture.

Price Waterhouse & Co.

Samuel Lowell Price founded an accounting practice in London in 1849. In 1865, Price partnered with William Holyland and Edwin Waterhouse, however, Holyland left shortly and in 1874 the firm was known as Price Waterhouse & Co. As result of increased business activity between the UK and the US, Price Waterhouse opened an office in New York in 1890. Price Waterhouse began to expand world-wide with separate partnerships in each country practicing as a federation of independent firms.

Formation of the Big Four (Initially the Big Five)

In the latter half of the 20th-century, pressure was building on the accounting profession to continue to grow and to maintain or increase profitability. Auditing of financial statements had become a commodity subject to extreme pressure on audit fees. To combat this, accounting firms expanded their advisory practices or branched out into other practice areas including management consulting, installation of computer based ERP systems, profit improvement studies, mergers and acquisitions and litigation support to name a few.

Additionally, there were four mergers among the Big Eight accounting firms, and ultimately one firm's demise to create the now existing Big Four. Based on pressure from the SEC and others, some of the accounting firms initially spun off, sold or discontinued their management consulting practices. They have now reinstated management consulting and related practices, however, some of these services cannot be offered to their audit clients.

Following is a summary of the mergers and the current size of the merged firms.

KPMG

In 1917, Piet Klynveld started in accounting firm in Amsterdam. He later merged with Kraayenhof to form KlynveldKraayenhif& Co.(KK &Co.) In 1979, KK &Co., Thomas McClintock in the US and a German firm Deutsche Truehandgesellschaft merged to form a strong European-based international practice called KMG. Dr. Reinhard Goerdeler was a chairman of KMG and is credited with laying the foundation of the Klynveld Main Goerdeler merger. In 1987 KMG and Peat Marwick joined forces to form KPMG in the US and other countries and Peat Marwick McClintock in the UK. In 1990 the name changed to KPMG Peat Marwick and in 1999 simply to KPMG. This was the first of the mega mergers and KPMG is now one of the Big Four.

KPMG employs 145,000 people and is headquartered in Amstelveen Netherlands. Their revenue was US$ 23 billion in 2012. In 2001 KPMG sold its US consulting firm, KPMG Consulting Inc. via a public offering. Its name was later changed to Bearing Point, Inc. which filed for bankruptcy in 2009. KPMG offers financial and regulatory audits tax services and advisory services. They still have a significant consulting practice, mainly to non-audit clients.

In 2007, several member firms in Europe, Asia and the Mideast including the UK merged to form KPMG Europe LLP. They have their own chairman and are headquartered in Frankfurt, Germany.

Deloitte

In 1989 Deloitte Haskins & Sells merged with Touche Ross to become Deloitte and Touche, later simply called Deloitte. Deloitte employs 193,000 people and is headquartered in New York. Revenue in 2012 was US$31.3 billion. It is reported to have the largest number of clients among the FTSE stock index of 250 companies. They are in over 150 countries.

Services offered include audit, tax and a variety of consulting services. Globally, Deloitte consists of separate member firms in each country, each of which is part of Deloitte Touche Tohmatsu, a UK company.

Ernst & Young

Ernst and Whinney and Arthur Young & Co. merged in 1989 to become Ernst & Young. They employ 167,000 people and are head-quartered in London. Revenues in 2012 were US$ 24.4 billion. Services offered include audit, tax, advisory and transaction advisory services. They operate in over 140 countries. In 2011, Forbes Magazine said they were the 8th largest private company in the US. In May 2000, Ernst & Young was the first firm to formally separate out its consulting practice by selling it to Cap Gemini for $11 billion in stock. Its global structure is organized into four areas based on geography.

PricewaterhouseCoopers (PwC)

The firm was created in 1998 by a merger between Price Waterhouse and Coopers & Lybrand. The merged firm employs 180,000 people and is headquartered in London. Revenue in 2012 was US$ 31.5 billion. PwC has offices in 771 cities and 158 countries.

Services offered include audit, tax and advisory services which includes performance improvement, transaction services, corporate finance, actuarial, and risk assessment.

Arthur Andersen & Co.

Arthur Andersen never had any significant mergers in the U.S. In the late 1980s, its management consulting arm, Andersen Consulting was growing faster than the audit group and it was more profitable. In 1989, Andersen Consulting and Arthur Andersen became separate units of Andersen Worldwide. This allowed Andersen consulting to retain more of its profits even though it shared a small percentage of them with the audit division, Arthur Andersen.

In the 1990s, Andersen Consulting sought and won an arbitration for the right to completely separate from Arthur Andersen and Andersen Worldwide.. They had to pay US$1.2 billion to the audit firm and couldn't use the name Andersen. In 2000 they split from Andersen Worldwide and changed their name to Accenture.

In connection with its Enron audit, the firm was indicted and subsequently convicted in 2002 of obstruction of justice for allegedly destroying documents related to the audit. This conviction of a felony prevented the firm from performing audits of public companies and it terminated its business. Most of the worldwide practices and its 85,000 employees were amalgamated into the four remaining accounting firms.

In 2005, the Supreme Court of the United States in a unanimous 9-0 decision overturned the conviction of the firm based on faulty instructions given by the presiding judge, to the jury to break the impasse of a hung jury.

Based on the Enron problem and several other financial statement inaccuracies in some other public companies, Congress passed in 2002 the Sarbanes Oxley Act to strengthen the audit function of public accounting firms. The Act created the Public Company Accounting Oversight

Board (PCAOB.) See Chapter Twelve for more information on the PACOB.

It also required public accounting firms to audit the internal controls over the preparation of public company financial statements to assess that adequate procedures are in effect to reasonably assure their accuracy. This increased the size of the market for audit services provided by public accounting firms. It also required that the CEO and the CFO of public companies include an opinion signed by them in their annual report that they believe appropriate procedures are in effect to provide reasonable assurance that their financial statements are free from material misstatements. It also stated what non-audit services could not be performed on audit clients.

Appendix Five

Auditor's Report on Financial Statements

The Board of Directors and Shareholders of XYZ Company, Inc

We have audited the accompanying balance sheets of XYZ Company, Inc as of December 31, 2012 and 2011, and the related consolidated statements of operations, cash flows and comprehensive income for each of the two years ended December 31, 2012. These financial statements are the responsibility of the company's management. Our responsibility is to express an opinion on these financial statements based on our audits.

We conducted our audits in accordance with the standards of the Public Company Accounting Oversight Board. These standards require that we plan and perform the audit to obtain reasonable assurance about whether the financial statements are free of material misstatement. An audit includes examining, on a test basis evidence supporting the amounts and disclosures in the financial statements. An audit also includes assessing the accounting principles used and the significant estimates made by management, as well as evaluating the overall financial statement presentation. We believe that our audits provide a reasonable basis for our opinion.

In our opinion, the financial statements referred to above present fairly, in all material respects, the financial position of XYZ Company Inc. at December 31, 2012 and 2011, and the results of their operations and their cash flows for each of those years, in conformity with US generally accepted accounting principles.

We have also audited, in accordance with the standards of the Public Company Accounting Oversight Board, XYZ Company Inc.'s internal control over financial reporting as of December 31, 2012, based on criteria established in Internal Control- Integrated Framework issued by the Committee on Sponsoring Organizations of the Treadway Commission and our report dated February 15, 2013 expresses an unqualified opinion thereon.

Houston, Texas   Able Auditor
February 15, 2013

Appendix Six

Auditors Opinion on Internal Controls

To the Board of Directors and Shareholders of XYZ Company, Inc.

We have audited XYZ Company Inc.'s internal control over financial reporting as of December 31, 2012, based on criteria established in Internal Control -- Integrated Framework issued by the Committee of the Sponsoring Organizations of the Treadway commission. (COSO) XYZ Company Inc's management is responsible for maintaining effective internal control over financial reporting and its assessment of the effectiveness of internal control over financial reporting is included in the accompanying Management's Report on internal control over financial reporting. Our responsibility is to express an opinion on the company's internal control over financial reporting based on our audit.

We conducted our audit in accordance with the standards of the Public Company Accounting Oversight Board. These standards require that we plan and perform the audit to obtain reasonable assurance about whether effective internal control over financial reporting was maintained in all material respects. Our audit included obtaining an understanding of internal control over financial reporting, assessing the risk that a material weakness exists, testing and evaluating the design and operating effectiveness of internal control based on the assessed risk, and performing such other procedures as we considered necessary in the circumstances. We believe that our audit provides a reasonable basis for our opinion.

A company's internal control over financial reporting is a process designed to provide reasonable assurance regarding the reliability of financial reporting in the preparation of financial statements for external purposes in accordance with generally accepted accounting principles. A company's internal control over financial reporting includes those policies and procedures that pertain to the maintenance of records that in reasonable detail accurately and fairly reflect the transactions and dispositions of the assets of the company, provide reasonable assurance that transactions are recorded as necessary to permit preparation of financial statements in accordance with generally accepted accounting principles, and net receipts and expenditures of the company are being made only in accordance with authorization of management and directors of the company, and provide reasonable assurance regarding prevention or timely detection of unauthorized acquisition, use or disposition of the company's assets that could have material effect on the financial statements.

Based on its inherent limitations, internal control over financial reporting may not prevent or detect misstatements. Also, projections of any evaluation of effectiveness to future periods are subject to the risk that control may become inadequate because of changes in conditions, or that the degree of compliance with the policies or procedures may deteriorate.

In our opinion, XYZ Company Inc. maintained, in all material respects, effective internal control over financial reporting as of December 31, 2012 based on the COSO criteria.

We have also audited in accordance with the standards of the Public Company Accounting Oversight Board, the 2012 financial statements of XYZ Company Inc. and our report dated February 15, 2013 expressed an unqualified opinion thereon.

Houston, Texas   Able Auditors
February 15,2013

Appendix Seven

Basic Business Functions

Every business has certain basic functions, almost regardless of the type of business. It also has a core or key function which is why it exists. Core functions can be described as its operation, or basic business purpose. It could be manufacturing a product, either consumable or non-consumable. Examples of consumables would be baby diapers, printer cartridges, packaged foods, cosmetics or over-the-counter medicines. Non-consumables would be automobiles or trucks, appliances, computers, cell phones, etc.

It could also be delivering a service such as designing and installing an ERP system, providing legal, accounting or auditing services, providing medical or hospital care, or offering repairs or maintenance services.

Examples of other basic core functions include retailing, wholesaling, energy exploration, production and delivery, transportation and construction. These functions can generally be described as the operation or operations of the business. All of these businesses generally need support functions, such as marketing, sales, accounting and human resources.

Marketing

Marketing involves determining who the market is for the company's products or services, determining how to appeal to that market, and focusing on how to sell to the identified market. It involves all aspects of creating a company image that makes it appealing to potential customers. Branded products have a brand manager who is responsible for the ultimate sales of the product, its market share, and its sustainability. Pricing and promotional discounts are also part of the marketing of the product.

Advertising is usually a component of marketing. It communicates the value and the presumed need for the product to the potential customer. Marketing is critical to the ultimate success of any product or service.

Sales

Selling is the act of meeting with customers, and convincing them to buy the product or service. Selling is usually done by sales people who are highly incentivized to maximize their selling activity by being compensated based on performance through commissions or bonuses. Sales can also be accomplished by selling from television ads and from internet selling.

Good salespeople are usually well-paid, sometimes earning more than some top management personnel in their company.

Accounting

Every company, profit or not-for-profit, has to have or should have an accounting department or function. Accounting involves the processing of sales invoices, paying vendors invoices, preparing payroll along with keeping the basic records. More important is the timely preparation of monthly internal financial statements, including an income statement, a balance sheet and a cash flow statement. For public companies and others with owners separate from management, or to meet regulatory requirements, accountants must also prepare external financial statements.

Accountants are also responsible for preparing income tax returns, sales tax returns, and many other regulatory returns, depending on the type and nature of the business.

Human Resources HR

This function has become more important recently as antidiscrimination and sexual-harassment issues seem to become more prevalent. Hiring and interviewing are usually handled by an HR department. The department is also responsible for maintaining personnel records covering salary adjustments and performance reviews. HR is also responsible for administering any health insurance or benefit plans, 401(k), or retirement plans and holiday and vacation benefits.

Certain companies also have research and develop functions, real estate departments, and legal departments.

About the Author

Bob Grottke was born in Oak Park, Illinois. He attended elementary and high school in the western suburbs of Chicago. He graduated from Northwestern University with a B.S. degree and an accounting major. He subsequently passed the CPA exam.

He worked his way through college first selling vacuum cleaners and then selling ladies hosiery, lingerie and other items of clothing door to door. Based on those experiences, he wrote a book called "All I Needed to Know in Life I Learned Selling Door to Door."

He then joined one of the big eight public accounting firms, Arthur Andersen & Co., where he spent 39 years, 26 as an audit partner. In addition to traditional audits, mainly in retailing, distribution and consumer packaged goods companies, he was involved in numerous special projects.

He was partner in charge of a team engaged by a committee of grocery retailers and grocery manufacturers to determine the cost to grocery retailers of accepting a coupon from a customer, and subsequently processing it for reimbursement from the issuing manufacturer. At the time of the first study, manufactures were paying the retailers two cents for each coupon redeemed, plus the face amount. Over a period of years, with a study being conducted approximately every 6 to 8 years, the handling fee increased from two cents to eight cents which it currently is today. At the time that most of these studies were done, for each penny paid per coupon redeemed, approximately $40 million annually was paid by manufacturers to retailers.

He developed a method for scheduling retail store employees based on productivity standards and sales forecasting techniques. This improved customer service by scheduling cashiers when needed, and it also reduced costs to the retailer. He was also involved in the development of a fresh meat reporting and control system for grocery store meat departments.

He headed a team that conducted a series of studies of pilot companies in the wholesale distribution industry directed to determining how to improve profitability. Based on this experience, he co-authored a book "Improving Productivity and Profits in Wholesale Distribution, the Magnifying Glass Technique."

While in public accounting, he developed and was editor of a semi-annual publication, "International Trends in Retailing," The publication reported on retailing activities in over thirty countries. It also featured success stories of leading retailers mostly as told by their founders or someone close to the founder. Examples include Franklyn Stores, Hy-Vee, J. Sainsbury, Crate & Barrel, Price Club, Ahold, IGA Inc., Tesco, Wal-Mart and Walgreens..

After retiring from public accounting, he spent 10 years as a financial consultant, working mainly with companies involved in the supermarket industry. He was an expert witness in several significant legal cases during that time

He then was elected Chief Financial Officer of IGA, Inc., an international organization, that supports and sponsors grocery retailers throughout the world. As CFO, he completely revamped and redesigned the accounting and reporting system, and installed a new ERP system. He is now retired from that position.

He is a member of the American Institute of Certified Public Accountants, the Illinois Society of Certified Public Accountants and a former member of the Institute of Industrial Engineers.

Bibliography

American Institute of Certified Public Accountants (AICPA) Website

Financial Accounting Standards Board (FASB) Website

Generally Accepted Accounting Principles (GAAP) Wikipedia 10/03/12

FASB Accounting Standards Codification News Release 07/01/09

2012 Financial Report of the United States Government

2011 Financial Performance Report and Overview of the Consumer Packaged Goods Industry (CPG) by the Grocery Manufacturers Association (GMA) and PwC.

National Association of Wholesalers (NAW) Website

Find-A-Code, Medical Billing Codes Website

American Health Information Management Association (AHIMA) Website

Public Utilities Commission Wikipedia 03/14/13

Independent Petroleum Association of America Website

Film production, wordpress.com 02/10/09

Cow-Calf Operations/ Confessions of a Pioneer Woman/ReeDrumond 04/12

AICPA Plain English Guide to Independence July 1, 2010

Public Company Accounting Oversight Board (PCAOB) Website

PCAOB Strategic Plan 2008-2013 03/31/08

KPMG Defining Issues, New PCAOB Standard on Internal Control Over Financial Reporting, 05/07 No. 07-16

PCAOB History

PCAOB Auditing Standard No. 5

Financial Accounting Foundation (FAF) Website

Internal Control-Integrated Framework COSO Website

Securities and Exchange Commission (SEC) Website

A History of Accountancy in the United States Gary John Previts& Barbara Dubris Merino, 1998

The Development of "the Big Eight" accounting firms in the United States, 1900 to 1990 The Accounting Historians Journal Vol 19, No1 June 1992

Peat Marwick, Mitchell & Co. 80 Years of Professional Growth, Speech by Walter E. Hanson at the Newcomers Society, 1978

business history.com/ind.-accountancy. php

History of the Major Accounting Firms, suite 101

Charles Waldo Haskins: The First Trusted Professional by Melissa Hoffman Lajara – NYSCCPA

E.W. Sells Awards aicpa.org 2011

Deloitte Haskins & Sells simplified family trees complied by Peter Boys

Deloitte ToucheTahmatsu International Information from Answers. com

KPMG Website

Deloitte Website

Ernst & Young Website

Ernst & Young firm profile

PwC Website

Arthur Andersen & Co. Encyclopedia of Chicago

Who Made America / Innovators/ Samuel Insull

Big Four (audit firms) Wikipedia 02/25/13

Made in the USA
Coppell, TX
26 April 2020